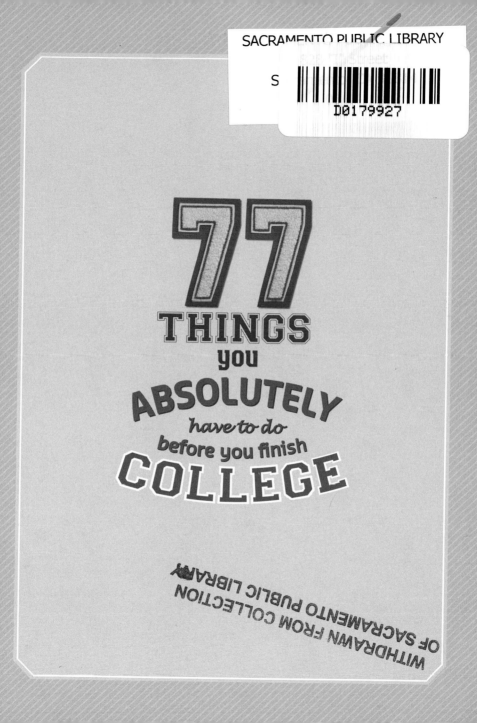

77
THINGS
you
ABSOLUTELY
have to do
before you finish
COLLEGE

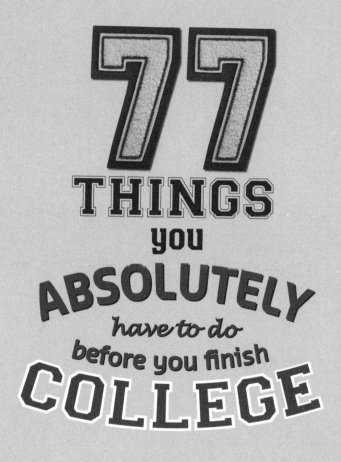

77 THINGS you ABSOLUTELY have to do before you finish COLLEGE

Halley Bondy

ZEST BOOKS

35 Stillman Street, Suite 121
San Francisco, CA 94107
www.zestbooks.net

Young Adult Nonfiction / School & Education
Library of Congress control number: 2013951194
ISBN: 978-1-936976-00-3

COVER DESIGN: Barbara Genetin and Theresa Currie
INTERIOR DESIGN: Dagmar Trojanek and Theresa Currie

Manufactured in the U.S.A.
DOC 10 9 8 7 6 5 4 3 2 1
4500457482

CONNECT WITH ZEST!
zestbooks.net/blog
zestbooks.net/contests
twitter.com/zestbooks
facebook.com/zestbook
facebook.com/BooksWithATwist
pinterest.com/zestbooks

Dedication

Gus, Luke & Max.
College, watch out!

Acknowledgments

Thank you, Tim Corbett, for the late-night lectures on how to build things, and thank you, strong Barnard women, for all the hard lessons.

CONTENTS

Introduction

Freedom! **Precious freedom!** Parental oversight has been discontinued, curfews are a thing of the past, and all those nightmares about forgetting your homework? Well, some things never change.

But you're in college now, and certain perks come with the territory: You can live on your own, buy stuff, vote, plan your future, party every night, make new friends, apply for internships, choose a major, and travel around the world. With so many new possibilities, it can be hard to know where to start. College can be one of the most exciting times of your life, but the freedom these years provide can also be a little overwhelming. On the one hand, you're thrust into independence like you've never experienced before (which is awesome!). But on the other hand, you're taking classes that are completely different, and often more difficult, than anything you took in high school, and you're more broke than you ever imagined possible (which sucks!). College wouldn't be college if it didn't include a wide range of experiences, from inspiring classes to terrible professors, from life-changing relationships to inedible dining hall food. Making sure you get the most out of these experiences is where *77 Things You Absolutely Have to Do Before You Finish College* comes in.

Whenever you're in need of a study break (or maybe even when you're not), open up this book for ideas to help you change things up and try something new. You might not get around to doing *all* 77 things, but you can pick and choose, browse, or tally up which of the 77 you've accomplished by graduation. From climbing rocks to pranking your friends to building your career to providing the soundtrack to the most raging party on your dorm floor, *77 Things You Absolutely Have to Do Before You Finish College* has you covered.

They say that life is what you make it, and the same goes for college. So make it unforgettable.

ONE Around the Pad

1 *Throw out*
the stuff you don't need

You're about to embark on a whole new life phase: "You: The College Years." Do you *really* need that camp T-shirt from when you were ten? Or that 'N Sync poster from seventh grade? Probably not.

Old items have a way of sticking around a lot longer than they should. Sure, some have serious sentimental value—like a family heirloom or a photo of high school friends. Then there's the random junk you'll never use again—like those ratty old pants that became highwaters long ago or the collection of Lisa Frank erasers that you just . . . *have*. This stuff, if hauled from your parents' house to your dorm room to your apartment and beyond, will take up precious space and keep you from getting newer things you really want.

Setting aside a couple of hours to bid adieu and toss out old junk will give you a surprising sense of calm and accomplishment. So roll up your sleeves and start sorting out the good, the bad, and the weird.

➤ HOW TO DO IT

Block out some time in your schedule, put on some good music, and clean out all the nooks and crannies where junk hides—drawers, boxes, forgotten storage bins, under the bed. Put everything in plain sight and then commence sorting. It helps to divide things into piles according to need.

1 / Definitely need

2 / Might possibly need

Or . . . donate!

Some of your expendables are headed for the trash no matter what, like worn-out shoes or notebooks full of freshman year's world history notes. But some things are likely in nice enough condition to donate to someone who needs them. Check out the local Salvation Army, Goodwill, or local donation drives (commonly run by churches and community centers), to find out what, where, and when items will be accepted.

3 / Probably wouldn't miss it if I never saw it again

4 / No way I ever need to see this item again in my life

Shove piles 3 and 4 into garbage bags (or recycling bins) and say good riddance!

After tossing out the junk, wait a week and review pile number two. Anything you can get rid of? Do it. It'll be easier the second time around. While you're at it, recall if you've even *thought* about the stuff in piles 3 and 4. The answer will probably be no way. (There's a life lesson in there somewhere.)

2 *Convert* your dorm room into your personal temple

Your room is your solace. You have to wake up there, work there, and crash there at the end of a stressful day. A gloomy, stark, cramped dorm room can put a damper on your mood. Imagine what it would be like to open your door and feel genuine relief, rather than "Ugh, this place again."

While you may not be able to change some aspects of your living situation—for example, your roommates or the lack thereof —you can take some simple steps to make your room your personal temple. In some cases, you don't have to spend a dime. In others, you can find cheap ways to upgrade your space.

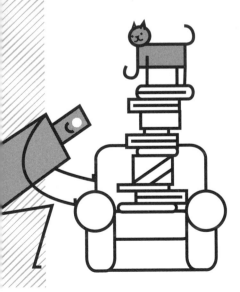

➤ HOW TO DO IT

1 / REARRANGE. Sometimes the path to a refreshing, open room is simply a matter of rearranging the furniture you already have. Make some space to open up the room. Create natural walkways, and try not to cram furniture together in one area. If your furniture is heavy, draw a map of the room and sketch different arrangements on paper first. Experiment with a few arrangements before settling on one, and purge the items you don't need. (That is, the items that you don't need and that actually belong to you. This is not a license to trash your roommate's favorite beanbag chair without her previous consent.)

2 / ADD COLOR. Bright greens, reds, yellows, oranges, or purples might sound tacky (and in excess they certainly can be), but unlike darker, muted colors, a single splash of vibrant color can transform your whole room. You can add a pop of color with a bright blanket on your bed, a throw rug, a painted nightstand, curtains, or decorative lanterns. Too much color might give you a headache, so start with one item and see how you feel.

3 / GET ARTSY. A piece of art can define a room. Framed art is especially convenient; it takes up no space, it classes up an otherwise plain wall, *and* it can be an expression of your personality. Many websites sell cheap poster reproductions of famous works of art, so you can hang a copy of that masterpiece you studied in art history in your very own abode. Classy.

How about a temple-temple?

If you're a spiritual person and you're looking to build an *actual* temple space like a Buddhist or Christian shrine or a place to do yoga or meditate, you might have to get creative. Convertible storage solutions (like a trunk that also serves as an extra seat for visitors) and portable furniture (like a wheeled bed) can give you the space you need to roll out your yoga mat and practice your downward-facing dog.

4 / LIGHTING IS EVERYTHING. Sunlight is essential to improving your mood, so hang lightweight curtains that will let in as much light as possible. But when the sun goes down, don't settle for the harsh glow of those horrible fluorescent lights that still dominate most college buildings. Play around with chic stand-alone lamps, soft reading lights, or Christmas lights to give your space a cozy warmth.

Find and rent an apartment

One of the biggest steps to adulthood is ditching dorm life and getting your first apartment. Signing a lease or rental agreement is a huge commitment, but adult life is full of huge commitments, and the sooner you start learning the ropes, the better. Plus, the additional freedoms that an apartment provides are priceless.

Unlike in the dorms, in your own apartment you'll have more control over your roommates, your location in town, the layout of your place, the bathroom situation, the cleanliness of the kitchen, and how much noise, or silence, you want around you. Take your time with this first search. That way you'll have the best chance of finding a place you really want, and you'll make it that much easier the second time around (which tends to sneak up on people faster than they usually think!).

➤ HOW TO DO IT

1 / GET YOUR FINANCES IN ORDER. Make sure that you can actually *afford* an apartment—and that it makes financial sense relative to what your college charges for housing. If it's a smart and viable money move, calculate what you can afford to pay each month, whether your folks will chip in, and whether your potential roommates will reliably cough up their share. You'll probably have to pay first and last month's rent and a security deposit up front. The deposit will be returned as long as there's no damage to the apartment when the lease is up.

2 / CONSIDER YOUR NEEDS. Write down your requirements and your preferences: location (close to school, grocery stores, good coffee shops), price range, number of bedrooms, and terms of lease or rental

Scam warning signs

You might be getting scammed if you notice the following:

* Your broker won't show you his or her license or references and asks for a cash fee up front.

* The landlord won't show you certain areas of the apartment or seems evasive.

* A broker's website looks sketchy or lacks details.

* A building doesn't seem legally residential (for example, it looks like a warehouse with padlocks on the doors).

* The lease is full of hidden fees.

THE SOLUTION: Always bring someone experienced along for a second opinion.

agreement. Do you want to be obligated to stay in a place for a year? Six months? Month to month? A summer sublet?

3 / GO ON THE HUNT. You can find apartment rentals through online listings or (in especially competitive real estate markets) through local real estate brokers. Bear in mind that going through a broker usually involves paying a fee, but it will save you the work of finding a place all by yourself.

4 / BE PICKY. See as many apartments as you can before making a decision, and run your lease or rental agreement by a trustworthy, experienced source.

5 / SIGN ON THE DOTTED LINE. Even if you're financially independent, you still might need to list your parents as guarantors, which means they guarantee that they have good credit or make enough money to support you.

The whole process can be an expensive hassle, but the moment you get that apartment key, you'll feel a sense of triumph and freedom you won't get in the dorms. Farewell, RAs. Hasta la vista, communal showers. This place is all yours.

4 *Bring* your roommate a gift

So, you've met your roommate: that complete stranger (or strangers) who will be living, studying, and snoring right next to you for the entire length of the school year. Maybe you'll have a lot in common and form a lasting friendship, or perhaps you'll be at each other's throats every minute.

Either way, it doesn't hurt to give your roomie a simple, occasion-free present as a nice gesture . . . or as a peace offering, depending on the circumstances. There's nothing quite like getting an unprompted gift, and by spending a few dollars (or even no dollars, if you get creative), you could brighten your roommate's day.

College can be stressful enough without adding domestic unrest to the equation. Trust us: A happy roommate is a good roommate.

A bonding opportunity?

A gift could also be a good opportunity to bond with your roomie. If your relationship needs a little fuel, have a night out—your treat. Or, get an interactive gift that you can use together, like a board game or a used video game for whichever console you guys have lying around.

➤ HOW TO DO IT

Getting your roommate a gift depends largely on the nature of your relationship and your roommate's preferences. Unless you're very close friends, keep it light, thoughtful, and even a little funny. An expensive or labor-intensive present might make your roomie feel indebted or, worse, totally creeped out. Instead, think back to your inside jokes and random conversations, like that time she mentioned hating her shower flip-flops (hey, those are pretty cheap). Remember when he was really understanding that time you broke his cup? Get him a better one. Does she like to snack? Bring her some leftovers from a class party.

Whatever you get, offer it with grace and little ceremony—and don't expect anything in return. Your roommate will totally respect your giving nature, and maybe he'll forgive you for eating all his candy bars last week.

... Then (nicely) *ask* your roommate to get lost

Sometimes you need alone time. Whether or not you like your roommate, it's nice to get a breather once in a while. Maybe you want to have friends over without the roomie hovering around, or maybe you just need a little space to feel sane.

Instead of suffering in silence and feeling crowded, why not speak your mind? If you simply grin and bear it, you might grow resentful, which will cause even more problems. Honesty is the basis for any good relationship, especially one in which you're stuck living together in a room the size of a closet. Ask your roommate to go to the library for a few hours, or see if she's willing to spend the weekend at home with her folks (they only live twenty minutes away, after all!). And maybe there's something you can offer to do in return? If it works out, you'll feel the pathway of communication open up between you and your roommate, *and* you'll get some breathing room while she's away.

➤ HOW TO DO IT

Remember, this is your roommate's place, too. She doesn't *have* to leave, but she *might* be willing to do you a favor. So, approach carefully and graciously. Be sure to ask at least a few days in advance and have a specific time frame in mind. You may also have to sweeten the deal with a trade-off: You'll spend Wednesday evening in the library (while she Skypes her long-distance boyfriend) if she disappears on Monday evening (while you blast your music as loud as you want), for example. Check in periodically to make sure you're both happy with the arrangement. Schedules and priorities can change, and you'll both have to adjust.

The sexile

"Sexiling" is when you exile your roommate so you can get it on. Basically, the same rules apply, with these stricter parameters.

1 / Have a very clear sexile agreement in place. For example, you can kick each other out once a week without notice, as long as it's only for two hours and before midnight. Or no sexiling during finals week. Whatever works.

2 / In case of sudden sexile, make sure you both have somewhere to hang out or take a nap. It's not cool to force your roommate into temporary homelessness.

3 / Be particularly considerate if your roommate never sexiles you. That's gotta be rough.

4 / Never have your hookup sleep over when your roommate is around, unless there's an agreement in place . . . or perhaps an air mattress on the floor.

5 / As always, be safe!

Sometimes, though, you can't *ever* come to an agreement . . . on anything. If you're in a dorm and can't get through to each other and you're both at the end of your rope, you may want to talk to a residence hall administrator to help work it out, or maybe even switch rooms. College is too short to feel miserable in your own space.

Build a killer sound system

A lot of people settle for laptop speakers. They get the job done, but admit it: It's not exactly the Bose experience. What if you could put together a high-quality sound system— something that surrounds you with your favorite music or movies and pumps up the bass? Investing in a great stereo system will make parties more fun, movies more exciting, and even homework more bearable with a good soundtrack. Keep your system in good shape, and you can even take it with you from dorm to apartment to . . . wherever. Believe it or not, you can achieve all this on a small budget, with a little patience.

➤ HOW TO DO IT

There are a few ways to kick up the sound in your room.

1 / **THE SIMPLE ROUTE.** Add a subwoofer to that laptop speaker setup. It will instantly increase your sound quality.

2 / **THE FULL PACKAGE.** For surround sound that leaves laptop speakers in the dust, you can buy a single component, like a surround bar speaker (a long, skinny speaker) or a home theater package. These home theater sets aren't as high quality as separate components, and you likely won't be able to replace separate parts without buying a whole new set.

3 / **BIT BY BIT.** If you're looking for something *really* high quality and lasting, start building a sound system piece by piece. These days you can find a used receiver for cheap(ish) online, a subwoofer in a thrift store (plug it in at the store to make sure it works), and maybe some unused surround speakers in your parents' garage or from a friend's defunct band.

You want your receiver to have multiple inputs so you can run a computer, DVD player, Xbox—whatever you want to listen to—through the same system. Your speakers should be compact, since you're probably in a small room, and you'll likely move several times in the next few years.

Or . . . keep it to yourself

What's the cheapest, easiest solution to an amazing sound system that doesn't bother anyone? A good set of headphones! If you want great sound quality, but your roommate hates your music, good headphones—not just earbuds—can be a perfect solution. These days you can buy noise-canceling, studio-quality headphones for a decent price, so head to the nearest electronics store to check out the latest in headphone technology.

With these few components, you'll probably have one of the best sound systems on campus. Over time, you can replace each component with higher- and higher-quality name-brand stuff (like Orb Audio speakers and a Marantz receiver) until you've got a truly killer sound system.

Now all you need to do is untangle those wires.

7 Produce your own beats

Almost every electronic-based song starts with a producer. As seamless as your favorite song may sound, someone had to toil in the studio to make that mix happen. These days, getting started on your own electronic music or mixing existing samples is as easy as the push of a button. Though musicianship certainly helps, plenty of producers and DJs these days kick off careers armed with nothing but a laptop and a good computer program. There's no reason why you can't do it, too.

Producing your own songs is also fun, therapeutic, and challenging, and eventually you might create something awesome enough to share online or from behind the DJ booth at a party.

➤ HOW TO DO IT

Some audio-mixing programs, like Apple's GarageBand, are included with the purchase of a computer. There are also a few reputable production programs, including Logic, Ableton, and FL Studio, all used by celebrity DJs. You can buy these online as downloads. Some offer free, no-frills editions that are fine for beginners, and you can always upgrade later. Once you download a program, the first step is to tinker around and get to know the interface. It's usually pretty intuitive: your song basically looks like a long bar filled with different lines and

Copyright laws

Though the internet has become the Wild West of copyright infringement, you are exposed to legal liability if you use and distribute samples of other peoples' music without their permission. Some musicians are understanding if you send them an awesome remix of their stuff—in fact, quite a few production careers have been jump-started that way. However, it's important to be aware of the risks. Review the U.S. Copyright Act, or go to copyright.gov for more information.

colors representing all of the song elements (or sequences) you're using. A good way to start is to upload a file to the program—like a song from your hard drive or a recording of your voice. This will represent one sequence on the bar. You can then manipulate that sequence with the program's endless effects. You'll be amazed how different your voice sounds when you start throwing on the filters!

Next you can add beats or instruments provided by the program, all of which you can filter, move around, slow down, or speed up. The possibilities are endless.

Building an entire song this way can be a slow, tedious, and sometimes overwhelming process, and you probably won't create a masterpiece on the first try. But practice pays off, and you'll at least get some goofy tracks out of the early test runs.

8 *Learn* to prepare one meal perfectly

Knowing how to cook—*not* just how to make a bowl of cereal—is an empowering life skill, and an essential one. You have to eat, right? But unless you're studying the culinary arts, you probably don't have the resources (fancy knives, a gas stove, a real chef's hat) to master the kitchen completely. However, *anyone* can learn how to prep a much-loved meal, and prep it really, really well. Think how gratifying it would be to make your favorite foods for yourself and your friends whenever you want, without the hassle and expense of going to a restaurant.

➤ HOW TO DO IT

Here's how to be a master chef—for at least one meal.

1 / SCOPE OUT YOUR KITCHEN. Does it have everything you need, like a sink, refrigerator, and stove with oven? Will you be able to use the kitchen for a prolonged period of time? If so, you're in business.

2 / CHOOSE YOUR MEAL. Figure out what you want to cook, tally the servings needed, and find the best recipe. Recipes are available online, on Foodnetwork.com or Epicurious.com, for example, and you can find videos on YouTube of chefs preparing a meal from start to finish.

3 / HIT THE STORES. Shop for fresh ingredients, but remember that most recipes are relatively flexible, so don't panic if you can't find or afford something nonessential, like a certain spice or an out-of-season ingredient. If you're dealing with perishables, like produce or meat, check the sell-by date or do a quick Google search so you'll be able to tell when it's fresh and how to clean it.

4 / GET SUPPLIED. If your kitchen isn't stocked with supplies, such as frying or baking pans, measuring cups, colanders, pots, knives, or

Vegetable sauté

Here's a healthy recipe to try on your first time out. It serves four.

INGREDIENTS

2 tablespoons olive oil, plus more if needed
1 package (14 ounces) firm tofu, drained and cubed
4 cloves garlic, minced
$1/2$ red bell pepper, cut into long, thin strips
4 cups snow peas
$1/2$ teaspoon salt
$1/4$ teaspoon freshly ground pepper
Soy sauce

Heat the pan over medium-hot heat. When the pan is hot, add the olive oil. Add the tofu and half of the minced garlic. Using a spatula or wooden spoon, stir occasionally for about 5 minutes, or until the garlic is lightly browned. If the oil begins to sputter, step back and reduce the heat. Put the cooked tofu and garlic in a large bowl.

Return the frying pan to the stove top and add the remaining minced garlic, the bell pepper, and the snow peas. Add a tiny bit of olive oil if the vegetables start to stick to the pan. Stir the vegetables occasionally until they are tender. This should take just a few minutes. Add to the bowl containing the tofu and sprinkle with the salt and pepper. Stir gently to combine, and serve. Add soy sauce to taste.

EXTRA CHALLENGE: Replace the snow peas or bell peppers with another vegetable, or add another ingredient.

anything else the recipe calls for, you may need to spring for those, too. It's a big shopping trip, but you'll be able to use these items over again while you practice perfecting that meal. You can also hit up your neighbors for supplies and offer to share the meal with them when it's done.

5 / **FOLLOW THE RECIPE, AND ENJOY.** Remember, patience is a virtue: A meal almost never turns out perfectly on the first shot, and sometimes the right kinds of mistakes can make your food even tastier. Worst-case scenario is that you can always try it again tomorrow!

9 *Build*
a piece of furniture

You've been living in your dorm or apartment for a few weeks, and it feels like something's missing. There's nowhere to put your feet up when you lounge on the couch. When unexpected guests drop by, they have to grab a throw pillow and park on the floor. And that nightstand in the corner is simply too short to be of any use. You could easily go to Ikea to take care of these things, but why not build something yourself? You'll save money (as long as you don't need a giant workshop or a blacksmith's forge), and you'll love that piece of furniture all the more because you got your hands dirty. And why settle for what's available when you can design exactly what you want?

➤ HOW TO DO IT

Figure out what kind of furniture you want to build—you can get ideas from books, design blogs, Pinterest, or something you see in a friend's apartment. Then sketch out your vision. An initial drawing will help you keep a stable plan and allow you to visualize how the item will be constructed, especially when you're in the middle of the project and the whole thing looks like a pile of wood and nails.

The next steps depend on what you want to build. There are many ways to make furniture, ranging from simple DIY cardboard assembly to intricate woodwork to upcycling items you already have on hand. If you're a beginner, you should probably start simple and ask advice from a more expert builder. Once you've decided on a project, research and purchase the specific tools and materials you'll need to get it done. That way you won't have to drop everything in the middle of your project to run to the store for last-minute supplies.

Always exercise caution when you build: Wear safety goggles even if you don't think you need them, and cut away from yourself when using sharp cutting tools. Remember that experts spend an entire lifetime perfecting the art of building furniture, so if your project doesn't turn out exactly the way you imagined it, don't fret. Learn from your mistakes and keep practicing.

How to make DIY rope-hanging shelves

Need a place for your small books and knickknacks but don't have time to hammer all day? Here's a simple way to make handy shelves on a budget. These rope-hanging shelves are lightweight, attractive, and very cheap to build.

MATERIALS

Electronic stud finder (optional)
Pencil
Two hook screws
Level (or a leveling app on your smartphone)
Shelving boards or light pieces of wood (about three 12-x-24-inch
    boards should do the trick, but this will depend on the size and
    number of shelves you want)
Measuring tape
Small drill
1-inch spade drill bit
Four long lengths of strong rope, like Manila rope or white nylon rope,
    about ¾-inch thick

1 / In order to secure load-bearing shelves on thin walls, you'll need to use the wall studs. To find the studs, run an electronic stud finder along the wall until it beeps, then place a mark on the wall accordingly. (Alternatively, you can knock against the wall with your knuckles and listen for a stud. A hollow sound means that there is no stud, and a solid sound is the sign of a stud.) Unless you're in a very old building, the studs will most likely be a uniform distance apart, usually 14 or 16 inches.

TIP: If you have walls made of plaster or drywall, you'll want to use an anchor in the drywall instead of screwing your hook into the stud. If you're living in the dorms, be sure to check with your RA before screwing anything into the wall.

2 / Now screw your hooks into the studs. Make sure your screws are at the same height. Use a level, if necessary.

3 / Next, you need to figure out where to drill through each of the shelves so that the ropes will hang straight down. The distance between the studs determines how far apart the holes in the boards should be, so take a moment to match the shelves up against the studs and indicate that distance on the boards. Place marks in the four corners of each board, aligned with the stud-indicator marks and an equal distance in from each board's perimeter.

4 / Using the indicator marks on the shelving boards, drill four 1-inch holes through these marks with the spade bit. Drill each hole both down from above and up from below the boards to avoid jagged holes and splintering.

5 / Insert one length of rope through one hole in the corner of the bottom shelf, then tie an overhand knot on the underside of the shelf to hold it in place, leaving a few inches of rope hanging below the knot. On the rope above the shelf, measure the distance you want the space between shelves to be (for example, about 7 inches if you want the shelves to hold a 6-inch picture frame) and tie another overhand knot there. Slide the rope above the knot through the corner hole in the next shelf and continue until all three of the shelves are secured with knots. Repeat this process through the other three holes in the other corners of the shelves. Make sure you leave lots of rope length above the top shelf so you can hang the shelves.

6 / Now that you have four lengths of rope sticking out above the four holes drilled in the top shelf, you can tie the ends together to form two loops at the short ends, so that you can then hang the entire structure from the hooks you screwed into the wall in step 2. (You might want to knot each loop a few times so they really stay.) Hang your shelves from the hooks and, voilà! You're ready to put your stuff on display!

10 *Turn off*
the outside world

I t's Friday night, and your friends want to go out and party, but after a long week there's nothing you'd like more than to relax and have a quiet night in. Just you, yourself, and . . . ooh . . . Facebook!

Who *hasn't* had that inner conflict at one time or another? Problem is that it usually ends the same way: Before you know it, you're flipping through your friends' pages, seeing who went to the game, finding out who ended up at that house party, liking, commenting, texting—and hours later you realize that you've whiled away the whole evening on the internet.

Sometimes you need an evening away from electronics. It's no easy feat to turn off your phone and computer (let's face it, tweeting *is* basically as essential as breathing), and temptation is right at your fingertips. But the world won't end if you flip the switch for one night and keep your thoughts to yourself. Your friends won't forget you exist, you won't lose all your followers, and those Instagram photos will still be there tomorrow. In the meantime, you can kick back just like people did in the old days (like the '90s) and get some real *you* time in.

➤ HOW TO DO IT

Luckily, the steps for a one-night social media diet are simple. Log out of Facebook, Twitter, Gchat, or any other outlet you use on a regular basis. Then take a deep breath, and turn off your phone. If you want a challenge, turn off the TV, too. (Your Kindle and music don't count. Download that Chomsky and crank that volume!) You'll be amazed how easy it is to occupy your mind with things beyond the screen.

Emergency!

Sometimes, people really need to reach you. Friends get injured and need escorts, and family members fall ill. But you still don't need to ditch your social media–free evening. Before you start your off-the-grid experience, send a mass email to friends and family to tell them that you're unplugging for the night, but that in case of a dire emergency, they can reach you on your dorm landline, on your roommate's phone, or through your RA. If those options aren't available, keep your phone on, but instruct people only to contact you if they *absolutely* have to.

You can rearrange your room or, for that matter, accomplish any other task listed in this chapter. Pick up those knitting needles you've only touched once. Practice that guitar. Write the next great American novel.

If you get the itch to update a status or send your friend that hilarious YouTube clip you watched the other night, stop and ask yourself, Can it wait until tomorrow? Most likely it can. Breathe deep and move on.

11 *Take* care of a plant

O ne easy way to liven up a room is to fill a corner with a lovely plant. That boring dorm window, that ancient flooring, that ugly fire escape: All these eyesores need is a little homey greenery to spruce them up, and you don't even have to dig deep in your pockets! Depending on the type and how sensitive it is, a plant can be a staple in your room for a long time. Some plants, like herbs or tomatoes, will give back more than visual beauty; you can eat them, too. Plus, compared to, say, taking care of a pet, a plant doesn't need all that much.

➤ HOW TO DO IT

You don't have to be a botanist to grow a plant successfully. Before you head to the local nursery, however, answer these simple questions.

- ➤ Do you want an indoor or an outdoor plant? Some plants survive better outdoors than in, but if you don't have outdoor space, you'll have to choose a plant that can grow indoors.

- ➤ How much sunlight do you get in the spot where you will put the plant? Different kinds of plants need varying degrees of sunlight.

- ➤ How often will you be around to water, feed, and maintain the plant? If you have a superbusy schedule or frequently go home on the weekends, you'll need a low-maintenance plant.

- ➤ How much space do you have for a plant?

- ➤ How long do you want the plant to last? Many plants are seasonal, or only live for a certain amount of time. Others, like some flowers, only bloom at certain times of the year.

- ➤ Do you want the plant to be green or popping with color?

Pesky pests

Unfortunately, you may not be the only one who loves your new houseplant. Aphids, mealybugs, and other pests can like it, too. Some can be harmful, while others are annoying and quick to breed. Ask the nursery expert about possible pest infestations that can affect your chosen plant and what you can do to control them—for example, by using an alcohol spray or traps, or by decreasing moisture to reduce fungus. If your plant becomes too infested to keep around, it's time to send it to plant heaven (aka, the trash).

An expert at a nursery can help you find the perfect plant based on your answers to these questions.

Once you've bought a plant, follow the instructions the nursery gives you. If you need to move it from sun to shade every week, write a note on your calendar. If you only need to water it once a week, let your roommates know so they don't drown it in an effort to be helpful.

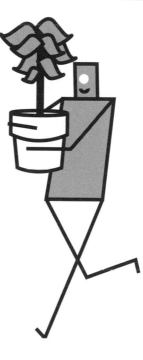

TWO Getting Out and About on Your Own

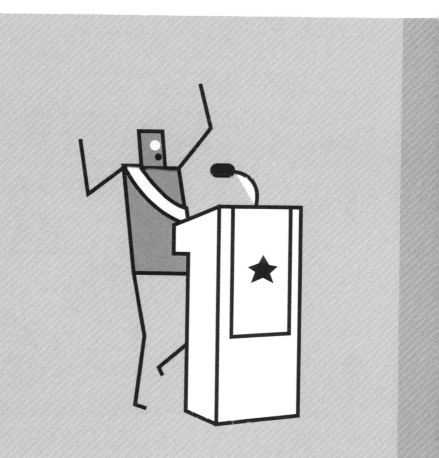

12 *Learn* some survival skills

I t doesn't hurt to know a few survival skills. Whether you're killing your food with your bare hands in a postapocalyptic world or sitting by a cozy campfire in a backyard, survival skills can be very handy when there aren't any amenities around. Those who hail from the country know that life without walls, stoves, or running water becomes a whole lot more bearable if you can *make* fire or *make* your own walls by way of a make-shift shelter, or if you can treat water for human consumption.

While it takes years to be a true survival expert, anyone can learn a trick or two to get by in difficult circumstances.

➤ HOW TO DO IT

The best way to learn survival skills is to seek out the experts. The many levels of outdoor preparedness range from tying simple knots to backpacking across a mountain range—so it helps to have an idea of what kind of survival skills you'd like to learn. If you want to go hardcore, check out established train-  ing institutions like the National Outdoor Leadership School, which hosts courses and excursions across North America. Or you can take a course in first aid at a local Red Cross. For simpler skills, your university or town likely offers a hiking club, a sailing club, a bird-watching club, a cartography club—any club that may pertain to the skills you're looking for.

How to pitch a tent

Knowing how to pitch a tent when you're camping is a priceless skill. It'll keep you warm, dry, and out of the reach of mosquitoes. But a tent right out of the bag looks more like a frustrating pile of poles and fabric than a sophisticated shelter. Here's how to keep from getting stuck in the rain.

1 / Choose a level site, and clear it of any sticks, rocks, or other obstructions.

2 / If your tent comes with a groundsheet, lay it out flat on the site.

3 / Position and spread out the tent on top of the groundsheet. If it's cold or windy, aim the window away from the wind. If it's hot or nice and breezy, aim it toward the wind.

4 / Lay out the poles. Usually you will have to slide the poles through sleeves or clips attached to the sides of the tent and into small metal grommets at each corner. Since each tent is different, however, be sure to follow the tent's accompanying instructions.

5 / Using the poles, lift and spread the tent into a taut position. Hammer stakes into the corner loops attached to the tent in order to keep it in place.

6 / For extra protection from the elements, attach the rain fly over the top of the tent. Make sure you line up the door and window flaps in the rain fly with the door and windows of the tent. Attach the ends of the rain fly to the stakes to pull it taut.

7 / Make sure water can't seep into the tent, like through the space between the groundsheet and tent. Fold the groundsheet along the side of the tent for protection.

13 *Talk* to an elder local

alking to the elderly is a time-honored form of community service, and for good reason. Some seniors are lonely, or they *love* telling stories from their past—and nearly everyone, young and old alike, enjoys talking about themselves, right? By offering your youthful ear to a local senior, you could make someone very happy for an afternoon. Plus, only a senior can answer burning history questions like these: How did dating *really* work in the 1940s? What did kids do for fun before TV or the internet? What was the password to the nearest speakeasy during Prohibition?

Who knows—their tales might help you appreciate your modern life all the more, or provide you with some helpful advice that you couldn't get anywhere else. You may even make a lasting friend or mentor.

➤ HOW TO DO IT

Talking to a senior is as easy as finding one. You can strike up a conversation with local characters, like that eighty-year-old eccentric grocer at the corner store or the old woman who feeds the pigeons in the park every day. If you're looking for a way to break the ice, try helping with something first, like carrying the person's bags or, as clichéd as it sounds, walking him or her across the street. Some chattier seniors might even strike up a conversation with you first.

A surefire way to find and engage a senior is to visit a local retirement home. Tell the administration staff that you want to spend time with the home's seniors, and they should be able to match you with a resident or two. The staff probably will love to have the help!

It's game time

Many seniors didn't grow up watching TV, so a lot of them love to play games. When you visit an elderly person, bring cards or a classic board game like chess to use as an icebreaker. If the senior lives in a retirement home that hosts group games like bingo night, consider sitting in on a round.

Remember: When speaking with seniors, you may need to be more patient. While many elderly people are sharp as tacks, others are hard of hearing or less socially aware than you're used to. Sometimes seniors process thoughts at the same speed you do, but they might not be able to express them as quickly as you can. Don't worry about the conversation going "right" or heading in a specific direction. Just sit back and enjoy spending time with someone new.

14 *Eat* something weird

Maybe you've been a picky eater your whole life, or maybe you grew up in a town where Outback Steakhouse was considered international cuisine (hey, it's Australian!). Either way, college is a time for new experiences, and one fun way to broaden your horizons is to eat something a little bit weird.

You might chow down on something you hated as a kid, only to find that your taste buds have evolved. You could try eating something unsightly, only to find out that looks can be deceiving. Or you might try a dish on the menu that you've never heard of.

Pushing yourself out of your comfort zone is a sure sign of growing up. Who knows? You may find that your limits aren't nearly as strict as you thought they were. And if worse comes to worse, you think the food is gross and move on.

➤ HOW TO DO IT

The word *weird* means different things for different people, but no matter how big of a foodie you are, there are always ways to try something different. Here are four.

1 / Pick a country on a map you know little about and eat at a local restaurant that serves that nation's cuisine.

2 / Visit a local farmers' market and look for a fruit, vegetable, or meat that you don't recognize. Ask the vendor about the best way to prepare it.

Weird food 4 u

If you want to push your limits, here are five seriously adventurous foods that you could track down and eat. Only the bold should apply.

* **DURIAN.** This fruit grown in Southeast Asia is known for its smooth, custardy texture and a smell so foul that the fruit is banned in some public spaces.

* **UGLI FRUIT.** True to its name, this Jamaican fruit looks like a battered, wrinkly, green-bruised orange. But if you can get past the outer shell, an Ugli fruit is a citrus treat, with a flavor somewhere between a lemon, a tangerine, and a grapefruit.

* **ROMANESCO.** This vegetable looks inedible, like rows of patterned seashells or some kind of nautical growth. But romanesco is a form of cauliflower, and you can prepare it the same way.

* **SQUID INK PASTA.** If you're not opposed to eating animal by-products, squid ink pasta is a lot more delicious than it sounds. Just like regular pasta, it's made of eggs and flour, but with the addition of the ink that stems from, to put it bluntly, squid butts. The result is a black color and a subtle briny flavor.

* **QUAIL EGGS.** They are exactly what they sound like: the eggs of quails. While they tend to be spotted and tiny, they function the same way regular eggs do. Only, you'll need to buy a lot more to make an entire omelet. (For a bigger challenge, eat them pickled!)

3 / Try something you think you hate, like pâté or steamed carrots, at a nice restaurant that's known for having a great chef. An expert chef might make the dish tastier than versions you've had before.

4 / If you're not ready to try a totally new food, alter your favorite dish. If you love chow mein, for example, try eating it extra spicy, or substitute chicken for tofu.

15 *Get* lost in town

It's easy to read guidebooks and go to the most popular lo-cal haunts. But after you've visited your city's most famous museum, eaten at the local ba-jillion-star restaurant, and gazed upon that stunning nature vista, what else do you do?

Another way to enjoy yourself is to head out *without* a goal. Take an aimless stroll around the place where you live—you'll have fun *and* make some new discoveries. You'll stumble upon weird surprises you can call your own: a cool, creepy antique joint, a hidden street with a funny name, a pet store whose owner lets you play with the puppies, or a surprisingly beauti-ful spot in an otherwise gritty city. There are treasures you can't find in any guidebook.

Record your findings

You'll want to remember your discoveries so you can share them with friends or come back to take photos. Here's a fun template for recording your findings.

WHAT IS IT? The abandoned Freemont Baseball Field

LOCATION: 33 West Drive, through the wooded area behind the gas station

WHY IT'S AWESOME: Great spot to hold an informal game. Also, feels haunted! Halloween party?

OTHER NOTES: Former home for the local high school baseball team before they moved to better facilities uptown. Closed after 8. The groundskeeper, Sam, is around during the day and tends the grass.

➤ HOW TO DO IT

This one's easy: The next time you have a free afternoon, start walking (or driving, as the case may be). Assign yourself a general direction and maybe a loose destination or two, but otherwise don't make a specific plan. Bring some cash in case you need to pay for food, water, or transportation, and head to an area that intrigues you. If you usually turn right at a certain corner, try turning left. Browse in a shop you always pass by. Read the historic plaques on the buildings or statues. If you find something interesting, explore it and ask questions if people are around.

Of course, "getting lost" isn't entirely literal here. You don't want to get truly lost, or wind up in an unsafe area by yourself. Every city is different, so exercise keen judgment. Only trek while it's light out. If you have a bad feeling about a neighborhood, steer clear. And bring your phone with you. While this activity can be very gratifying alone, you could bring a friend along for extra assurance. Safety in numbers!

16

Join a political campaign

Whether you're very politically active already or just slightly interested, joining a political campaign can be a fascinating experience. If you can devote a few months, weeks, or even hours to a campaign you believe in, you'll get to know the inner workings of government (and, yes, its problems) and learn how you can exact change in your city or town. Maybe you'll realize that you were born to run for office some day—or, you know, not.

Joining a political campaign is also a great networking opportunity. You'll be around smart, passionate, and professional people who will often be helpful contacts in the future.

➤ HOW TO DO IT

Here's how to find the right political campaign for you.

1 / PICK YOUR BRANCH. Presidential candidates aren't the only ones who need to campaign. You can get involved in congressional, board of education, town council, mayoral, county supervisor, and judiciary elections, too. Figure out if your interests lie on a more federal level, or if you'd rather be involved in a small-scale campaign with a more intimate crew of volunteers. The size of the campaign also depends on where you live: the mayoral election in New York City is a lot bigger in scale than in a rural town with a population of 2,000, for example.

2 / PICK YOUR CANDIDATE. Study the candidates and their qualifications and beliefs, and choose a candidate you believe in. If you're uncertain about a candidate, call or write to his or her offices with questions.

3 / REACH OUT. When you reach out to local campaign headquarters to get involved, make sure that you're dealing with the candidate's official campaign, not an offshoot group that may wander from the candidate's real interests. Depending on how organized the campaign is, you may be able to apply online for a volunteer position. Other elections might require a little research and a phone call or two before you can speak to someone about volunteering.

4 / BE HONEST. When you speak with the campaign organizer or fill out an online form, be realistic about the hours you can commit and what you're willing to do. You might be asked to do anything from envelope stuffing to flyer design to cold-calling strangers to raise funds. Outline your talents carefully and keep an open mind.

Give a tour to out-of-towners

At some point, you'll probably have out-of-town guests visit you at school. Sure, you could take them to local restaurants, show them your dorm, and have a totally nice time. But what if you did something completely different and gave them a real tour of the town you're living in? Not just a tour of your favorite pizza place, but a bona fide walking tour filled with facts about the local history, nature, and legends? Conducting a walking tour is your chance both to play guide and to learn more about your town.

Go pro?

If you love showing people around and want to spend more of your time doing it, consider giving guided tours as a part-time job. Whether you're a nature buff or you love your city's architecture, look into local sightseeing licensing laws and work your way toward becoming a full-fledged guide. It's a flexible, often lucrative gig, and you'll get plenty of exercise pounding the pavement (or the trail).

➤ HOW TO DO IT

Here's how to give the perfect guided tour.

1 / KNOW YOUR GUESTS. Before they come to town, take into account what they might be into. Are they into nature? War history? Oddities? Music? And how much would they be willing to walk?

2 / DO YOUR RESEARCH. Your goal is to find the best places and facts that will interest your guests. You can probably find a lot of information online, but to level up as a tour guide, you should go on at least one professional tour yourself, be it a city walking tour, an informative nature hike, or a guided museum visit. If you live in a small town without professional guided tours, you could track down a local historian who knows the ins and outs of the place and ask for tips.

3 / FOCUS ON THE FUN STUFF. You don't need to include every detail about every brick in every building. When planning your tour, outline a very general description about each stop or location and include two or three fun facts.

4 / BE FLEXIBLE. Your guests might want to rest a lot, or they might be interested in stuff way outside your planned tour. Let it happen. The idea is for everyone to have a good time, and maybe everyone will learn something in the process.

18 *Volunteer* at a shelter

More than 630,000 people are homeless in the United States, and your local shelter could probably use some extra hands. Many homeless shelters are underfunded and need volunteers to work in the kitchen, raise money, or help with other tasks. The people you'll meet come from all walks of life, and some have undergone major traumas, so the experience can be emotionally difficult for new volunteers. However, if you have an open, strong mind and a giving spirit, or if you're interested in the world of social work, this is a chance to directly affect the lives of people in need. You won't just be helping the people the shelter serves, you'll also be learning a lot about the world right outside your door.

Not a people person?

Animal shelters need volunteers, too. These facilities are always looking for dog walkers, cage cleaners, foster homes, and all sorts of help both inside and outside the shelters. Working in an animal shelter isn't for the faint of heart, though; many animals in shelters have been abused or traumatized, which can be extremely upsetting. And you'll have to restrain yourself from adopting every adorable animal in the place.

➤ HOW TO DO IT

You can find local homeless shelters online through the National Coalition for the Homeless (NCH) or Housing and Urban Development (HUD), and inquire about volunteer work. Some shelters don't have an online presence, so you may need to call for information. Once you get a shelter official on the phone, remember that there are countless ways to volunteer. Take a moment to assess your skills, commitment, and wants. Would you rather work face-to-face in the actual shelter, donate items, or lobby for the rights of the homeless on a governmental level? Address shelter staff with specifics: "I wanna volunteer" is far less helpful than "I'm a great cook, I'm good with people, I'm a heavy lifter, and I can commit weekends."

Once you're working in a shelter, get to know the place. Don't step out of your given role unless you have the go-ahead from an organizer. Many facilities, like battered-women's shelters, require extra training and paperwork (understandably) before volunteers can interact with the residents.

If you *are* charged with working with the residents, treat the people you encounter with empathy and a listening ear. Remember that genuine connections take time, so don't expect to make a huge impact on your first day. Keep coming back and helping a little bit at a time.

Go to a town/city council meeting

From streetlights to potholes to parking tickets, your local government keeps it all working. The mayor, town council, and other officials meet at least weekly to manage the city's operations, and as a resident, you're invited.

Sitting in on a council meeting will give you an entirely new perspective on your town. Street cleaning, tree planting, local parades—these things don't just *happen*. Human beings make each and every decision that goes into public works and events. Sometimes, planning goes well, and other times, the process is choppy, complicated, and even downright contentious. It's pretty exciting stuff, and if you're passionate about an issue in your town, a council meeting is your chance to hear from, and speak to, the source.

➤ HOW TO DO IT

There are bound to be issues you care about. Your favorite park is filled with trash, for example, or the town is taking away student-discount transportation privileges. These are great reasons to head to a council meeting and find out how the local government is handling your concerns.

The meeting schedule should be available online—all you have to do is show up. During a meeting, the mayor *usually* presides over the council (but this is not the case in some major cities), and the council goes over new legislation or business, such as building permits, parking regulations, tax rates, and wage increases for public officials. At the end, there is usually an open forum for anyone to speak, including you.

Towns vs. cities

There is an enormous difference between council meetings in big cities and those in small towns. A big-city council meeting will cover a broader scope of issues and will probably attract a much larger audience. The opposite is true for meetings in small towns. If you have a very specific problem in a huge city, like one pothole on one particular street, you'll want to talk to a district leader rather than a council member.

If you choose to speak, remember the scope of local government. A town council is charged with local public matters, not the federal government or what's going on inside private institutions. It's not a place to rave about the U.S. president or how the local McDonald's is treating employees. These are federal and private matters, respectively. Also, the council is usually separate from local public schools, which are handled by the board of education.

When you speak, be courteous, to the point, and brief. Don't rant on and on about an issue or criticize the character of council members—you want these people on your side. Encourage empathy, and you can help make change.

Have a meal out by yourself

Eating at a restaurant is usually a group activity, but believe it or not, getting a table for one isn't unheard of. It may seem awkward or strange at first, but eating at a restaurant by yourself—not a bagel place, not a Dunkin' Donuts, but a sit-down *restaurant*—can be a fun social challenge. You can have a nice meal in peace, read a book, and not have to bother with sharing your French fries. And there won't be any negotiating over the tip at the end of the meal. You'll probably find that eating solo isn't a challenge at all, but a well-earned respite.

What can you do?

Remember that the idea is to relax far away from your cares and worries, so leave the textbooks at home and consider turning off your phone. There are plenty of other ways to keep yourself entertained on a solo restaurant trip.

* Learn sudoku

* Finish that novel your uncle gave you last Christmas

* Write in your journal

* Draw

* Read an actual newspaper

* Formulate your plan for world domination

➤ HOW TO DO IT

Pick a restaurant you enjoy—like that place your friends never want to go to or the one that looks really, really cozy. The rest of the steps are pretty much the same as they would be any other time you go to a restaurant. Go up to the host and ask for a table for one. As self-conscious as you might feel being alone, brave through it. People are usually too engaged in their own conversations to judge you, and no professional waiter or hostess will look at you sideways if you eat alone, especially if you tip well at the end of the meal. So, sit back, relax, and bon appétit, solo style!

21 *Join* a (low-commitment) interest group outside school

Sure, your school has academics, sports, theater, and club programs. But your town probably has some version of these programs, too. Community theater, for example, or writers' groups, local sports teams, art-critique meet-ups, community Spanish classes, off-campus yoga groups, scientific-discussion groups, religious groups, political discussions—any number of these activities may be available to you off campus. While college is a great opportunity to indulge your interests, joining a group outside school will get you away from the same old campus faces and into a new place. You'll meet people from different ages and backgrounds, and unlike school clubs, these meet-ups could continue long after graduation.

➤ HOW TO DO IT

You're more likely to find a diverse sampling of meet-ups if you're studying near a big city, but it's not impossible to find your own community in a small town.

A lot of larger institutions—like community theaters, Mensa (if you can pass the admissions requirements, of course), or churches—typically have groups and meetings. Looser, informal meet-ups, like book clubs or small writers' groups, are usually found by word of mouth or through friends or social media. Websites like Craigslist or Meetup.com can help point you in the right direction.

When you make contact, ask if you can sit in on a meeting without becoming a member first. That way you'll get a feel for the club (or class, or troupe, or whatever) before you commit anything.

Or, DIY

Without a doubt, it's much easier to start a club on campus than off. But, if you want to be involved in the local community, you could organize an outside group. You should probably keep it small and loose, like a book club or an informal film-critique group. You don't want to go nuts dealing with expenses and meeting venues. This is supposed to be fun, after all.

If you like what you see and can make the time for it, sign up! You might be required to pay admission or dues, or offer a minimal time commitment, so find out the details before making it official.

However, if you feel a group is disorganized, uninteresting, filled with stupid people, or, worse, cultish, trust your instincts and steer clear before you pay up.

22 *Create* a photo collection

Most people take photos of their friends at parties, funny things they see on the street, or particularly tasty food. But why not take photos with a larger goal in mind? These days, you don't need to be a pro or own a superexpensive camera to create a photo collection you're proud of. If you head out with your camera or smartphone and a mission to create a photo diary or collection, you'll find yourself paying attention to your surroundings in a new way. You'll also learn a thing or two about lighting, framing, and manipulating images.

Later on, when you flip through your photos, those little things you saw—that rock, that kid in the park—will take on a whole new meaning. Plus, you can carry them with you forever, and even use some for a portfolio or website.

Ask away

For your photographic purposes, you shouldn't take photos of people unless you ask them first (or ask the parents if you're photographing a child). Approach politely, and tell them exactly how the photo will be used. If they say no, graciously walk away.

➤ HOW TO DO IT

If you're a novice, you can use a smartphone, which automatically adjusts its camera's focus and colors for you. However, if you can afford a good digital camera and think you'll use it beyond this collection, go for it. There are many different kinds of cameras, and the market changes every day, but fun novice cameras range from simple point-and-shoots to digital SLR (single-lens-reflex) cameras with interchangeable lenses.

Next time you're out and about, pay attention to the world around you. See what inspires you, and take some test shots. Choose a theme for your visual diary and create a coherent collection around it. Maybe the locals, the architecture, the dirty stuff, or the wildlife inspires you. Maybe your town would look completely different in black and white, or you have a friend or muse you want to photograph in different settings.

Once you've captured the images, you can use programs like Photoshop to crop, resize, filter, and manipulate the images to your liking, or even create a collage from the whole lot.

In the end, how you want to display your collection is up to you. Do you want to put it on your personal website? On Instagram? Do you want to submit it to a gallery? Or do you want to keep it all to yourself? The photos are yours to distribute, or not.

Spend quality time in the library ... without doing homework

There's nothing quite like a university library. Some are centuries-old monuments to architectural beauty, filled with historic texts and artifacts. Others are modern marvels, allowing you to do your research surrounded by sophisticated panes of glass and minimalist art. Still others are boring, cramped buildings that simply get the job done. But all contain massive amounts of information on a broad range of subjects, and more books than you can shake a stick at. Maybe you use the library as a place to hunker down and work when your dorm is too noisy or full of distractions. But have you ever thought of going to the library to do something other than homework? In an age when we can access anything we want at any time online, it's refreshing to stumble upon real, solid books by accident. Besides, once you graduate, you might not have access to the library anymore, so you may as well explore while you can.

➤ HOW TO DO IT

One way to go about exploring your library is to wander around and get lost, which can lead to exciting discoveries. Or, you could make a list of the coolest stuff on the library floor plan or in the catalogue before you start exploring. You can go on a hunt for a certain subject or pick the room with the craziest name and head in that direction. However you choose to explore, you might come across some fun oddities, like a twelve-volume series on calligraphy or a creepy, tucked-away room filled with rare sheet music. And man, does *Catcher in the Rye* look different when written in Greek!

The award for most books goes to . . .

Most schools have hugely extensive libraries. On the American Library Association's list of the one hundred biggest libraries in the United States, universities make up seventy-four of them. You could be attending a school with an enormous book collection and not even know it.

These are the ten American universities with the most extensive library collections, in order from biggest to smallest:

1 / Harvard University

2 / University of Illinois, Urbana-Champaign

3 / Yale University

4 / University of California, Berkeley

5 / Columbia University

6 / University of Michigan

7 / University of Texas, Austin

8 / University of Chicago

9 / University of California, Los Angeles

10 / Indiana University

To see where your school stands, visit the American Library Association website, ala.org.

24 *Take* a class that has nothing to do with your major

Once you choose a major, it's easy to get a sort of educational tunnel vision. There are certain classes you have to take to fulfill your credit requirements, and they're all kind of . . . the same. But college provides a rare opportunity to explore any field you want, even if you just want to do a little dabbling. Once you leave the campus life, the opportunity to take a survey course of something outside your specialty becomes harder and harder to come by. Now's the time to be daring and try something just for the heck of it.

Before you graduate, enroll in at least one class that has nothing to do with your major. Fulfilling your major credits is important, but so is satisfying your curiosity while you have the chance.

Or . . . join a club

If you have extracurricular interests but you can't spare the time or credits for a whole class, there may be an on-campus club you can join instead. That way, you won't have to worry about grades at all, and you can be involved when it works for you and your schedule.

➤ HOW TO DO IT

Maybe you're an earth science major, but you've always been a little curious about painting. Or you know you're destined for a life in the theater, but you're also pretty interested in marine biology. Does your school offer unusual, fun-sounding classes like the Science of Sleep or Blacksmithing that you're itching to try? If you can afford the credits, don't be shy. Enroll in a level-appropriate class, even if it doesn't count much toward graduation. You aren't worrying about credits—you're taking this class just because you want to.

Remember, though, that any new course is going to be a lot of work. You'll have to buy textbooks and possibly other supplies (if it's an art class or another studio class), make time for homework, and pass any tests or finals that are part of the syllabus. Taking a class for fun doesn't mean you can slack off, because the class grade will affect your overall GPA. If your GPA is too precious to risk, see whether your school offers a pass-or-fail option, which enables you to pass or fail a class without working toward a grade.

25 *Have* a real conversation with your favorite professor

If you have a professor you admire, now is your chance to get to know him or her, and for the professor to get to know you.

Once you leave college, you'll probably remember your favorite professor fondly. All that advice, those fiery lectures, those ridiculous jokes—they'll stick with you for years and years. The more time that goes by, though, the harder it will be to get in touch with him or her, and the more you'll wish you'd made a real connection when you had the chance.

Professors don't stop existing once class is over. They're professional contacts for the future. They're authors. They're noted experts in their field. Moreover, they're human beings. After dealing with classes full of hundreds of often-preoccupied students all day, they might relish the opportunity to chat with a student who is genuinely interested in the subject they care about enough to teach. Why not strike up a meaningful conversation?

Beware the brownnosing

Nobody likes a brownnoser. When you talk to a professor, don't overdo it with compliments or try too hard to impress. *Definitely* don't bring a gift. (It's usually against university policy for professors to accept gifts from current students, anyway.) Just be your bright, funny, friendly self and enjoy the conversation.

➤ HOW TO DO IT

Professors may seem too intimidating to approach, but, really, they don't bite. Start your quest by visiting a professor during office hours. Students often use these hours to talk about grades or deadlines, so a professor will probably welcome a visit with a higher conversational purpose.

Come in with something relevant and agenda-free to talk about, like a thoughtful question prompted by last night's reading, or a point you want to learn more about from today's lecture, or an idea you have for your next paper. The topic should be something that expresses your enthusiasm for the material in and of itself, rather than concerns about grades. Remember that you're trying to make a connection that goes beyond campus walls.

Unless he or she is a total curmudgeon (which does happen), your professor should appreciate your enthusiasm and might even be a little flattered that you sought out him or her. Maybe the conversation will go so well that you can do it all over again the following week. Eventually, the professor can recommend you for jobs, grants, fellowships, or other opportunities in your field. Regardless of what happens in the future, you'll have an interesting conversation with an intelligent person you admire—and that's a reward in itself.

26

Start an on-campus club

There's no denying that college is a wonderful place to expand your mind and discover new passions. But sometimes discovering those passions requires a little investment of time and energy from you and your fellow students. Starting an on-campus club is a great way to find people who are interested in the same things you are and explore those interests together. You can build a club around just about anything, from film appreciation to food appreciation, to speaking Klingon to quilting.

➤ HOW TO DO IT

If you want to start a club, here's how to do it.

1 / FIND SUPPORT. You'll want to gauge your fellow students' interest before you start a club. If you have a great idea but nobody wants to join, you might need to refine the club's purpose. Ask around and see who's interested.

2 / CONSULT THE SCHOOL. No matter what kind of club you want to start, consult your university about its policy on new clubs. You may have to register the club with your university or student government in order to use the facilities. Sometimes universities set aside funding for clubs, so ask if you'll have access to any aid.

3 / PLAN IT OUT. Consider the following questions: How many people should be in the club? How often will it meet? What will be on a typical agenda? How much money will be needed to operate? What kind of facilities and/or equipment will be required? Are there any rules for membership?

4 / KEEP COSTS LOW. Unless you have an endless supply of cash and time, you'll probably want to keep overhead and time commitment low. Club members (not to mention *you*) will be very busy with school, and even school-sponsored clubs tend to have limited funds. Try to keep meetings and activities as cheap and fun as possible.

5 / GET CONNECTED. When you're starting out, it can be helpful to link up with clubs at other universities to learn their methodology or even share resources. Many of these groups, like AIDS-awareness groups, work in tandem with organizations on and off campus, and even provide funding. Do some research and find out if you can meet at least a few times with some nearby organizations that are similar to yours.

How to win members

So you have a great idea for a new club, but you don't know how to find members. Draft a well-written, concise pitch that describes the club's purpose and get it out there! Send the pitch in an email to your friends, urging them to pass it on to anyone who might be interested. Post flyers around campus with clear contact information (as long as you have school approval to do so), and use social media to spread the word.

27 *Learn* a language you've never studied

You've probably been studying the same language for years already. Maybe you'll continue to study it in college, which is great! But, if you have room in your class schedule, why not learn a new language, too? Switch up your language classes by taking Mandarin or Hindi. (Incidentally, Mandarin and Hindi are spoken by way more people in the world than Italian or French.) Learning a new language is always a challenge, but studies show that once you've learned two languages, learning a third becomes easier.

➤ HOW TO DO IT

There are almost 7,000 spoken languages in the world, and your university probably offers more than a few of them. Here are some questions to ask yourself to narrow down your options.

➤ Is there a particular foreign country you'd like to visit or live in some day? If so, take a class in the local language. At the very least, you'll know how to order a meal and find the bathroom when you get there, and you'll probably pick up some very useful conversational skills, too.

➤ Do you want to take an easier language? Every language has its own challenges, but if you're an English speaker, the Romance

Fun language facts . . .

* English has one written script system: *a, b, c, d,* etc. Japanese, however, has three: kanji, hiragana, and katakana. They're often all used in the same written sentence!

* In parts of northern Spain and southern France, more than 700,000 residents speak an unusual language of unknown origin called Basque. Sentences like *"Pozten naiz zu ezagutzeaz"* (nice to meet you) and *"Zenbat da txartel bat San Sebastien ra"* (how much is a ticket to San Sebastián?) don't look very much like Spanish or French, do they?

* In the Ozark Mountain region of Arkansas and Missouri, the dialect contains traces of sixteenth-century English. Though the dialect has become one big blend over the years, residents use many antiquated words, including *sallat* for "salad" and *ruinate* for "ruin," both of which were used by Shakespeare.

languages (Spanish, French, Italian, Portuguese, and Romanian) are probably easier transitions for you than, say, tonal languages like Cantonese or Vietnamese. According to the U.S. Department of State, other "easy" languages for English speakers to learn are Afrikaans, Dutch, Norwegian, and Swedish. The hardest? Arabic, Cantonese, Mandarin, Japanese, and Korean.

➤ Do you want to study a language that a lot of people speak? UNESCO, a division of the United Nations, states that the most widely spoken languages in the world are Mandarin, Spanish, English, Hindi, Arabic, Portuguese, Bengali, Russian, Japanese, German, and French.

➤ Is there someone in particular you'd like to communicate with? Maybe you have a relative who only speaks Czech, or you think the Argentinian exchange student in your statistics class is really cute. Learning a few words or phrases in someone's native language is a great way to show that you care about his or her heritage.

28 Try a sport you've never (or barely) tried

Are you an athlete (or a wannabe one) looking for an alternative to your favorite sport? Are you stuck in the same old gym routine? Or maybe your routine consists of staying as far away from the gym as possible. Perhaps you have an interest in sports, but the closest you've come to getting out on the field is playing table tennis (which is, actually, an Olympic sport). If any of these scenarios ring true, you're in the right spot: College is the perfect place to try new sports, whatever your level.

Different sports work different muscle groups—which include parts of the brain that need a workout, too—so it's important to switch up your game now and again. Even if your school isn't famous for having a stellar sports program, you're probably surrounded by teams you didn't even know existed. Trying a new sport is healthy for your mind, body, and social life. And who knows—you might get hooked on polo (or whatever) for life.

➤ HOW TO DO IT

Football, soccer, martial arts, squash, track, kickboxing, and rock climbing—there are many different kinds of sports. Even yoga or Zumba fitness classes can function as sports, in that they'll help keep your body healthy and put you around like-minded people. Figure out what kind of physical activity you want to try. Many sports, like swimming, cycling, and dancing, are easily tailored for beginners. Others, like team sports, require a bit of experience.

Aside from official school sports teams, there are usually clubs, fitness classes, intramural sports, and even opportunities to play sports off campus. Consult your school activities office for ideas, or find the nearest gym to see what's available. You may even stumble upon something more informal, like a weekly ultimate Frisbee game in the park.

When you join up, tell the instructor, coach, or leader that you're a complete novice so he or she can take extra time to explain the rules or place you with other beginning players. If it's an informal group without professionally trained coaches, find a friendly player and explain that you might need some help getting up to speed. And have fun!

Just don't overdo it!

Taking on a new sport can mean aches and pains in muscles you never even knew you had. Some soreness is to be expected, but overdoing a new exercise routine without taking proper precautions (especially in an unfamiliar sport) can lead to more serious injuries. Here are some ways to avoid overdoing it:

★ Don't play a brand-new sport two days in a row.

★ Take the time to warm up—jogging lightly or performing the upcoming activity at a reduced intensity—before every game or strenuous exercise routine.

★ Drink plenty of water around the clock, and always bring extra to your games, practices, or classes.

★ If you're injured or in pain, don't work that area of your body.

★ Don't set unreasonable goals. Modify the workout or activity to your level.

Study abroad

Whoever came up with the idea of studying abroad is a genius. Studying abroad is a rare opportunity to break away from your usual routine and spend a semester, or even a year, in a foreign country. It's one of the easiest ways to travel because all of the details are taken care of by your university. Your housing and food will be prearranged. You'll use the country's textbooks and attend local university classes, where you'll be surrounded by university students just like you.

In the end, you'll leave more fluent in the local language if it differs from yours, and your personal growth will be boundless. Studying abroad is an excellent lesson in independence and adapting to new situations and customs. The world is much bigger than your college town. Who knows—maybe you'll fall in love with the place and want to return after graduation.

➤ HOW TO DO IT

Many students study abroad during their junior year. By then, you'll be settled in college life, and you'll have had a chance to study a language on a college level. (Some programs have a minimum language requirement.) You'll also get a lot of general education classes out of the way so you can use your time abroad to get a different perspective on the subject you're majoring in. Find out about the programs offered at your school by visiting the study-abroad office, which might go under another name, like the Office of International Programs.

Studying abroad is exciting and fun, but it's not a luxury vacation. You'll have to attend school and do homework, as at your college at home. You'll probably feel pushed out of your comfort zone as you learn your way around a new city and university and live a differ-

English only, please

If you haven't studied another language, visit any English-speaking country; many have excellent study-abroad programs. The UK and Canada are obvious choices, but English is an official language in countries you may not have considered. Here are some examples:

South Africa

New Zealand

Ghana

Belize

Trinidad and Tobago

Singapore

the Philippines

Tanzania

Jamaica

Malta

ent lifestyle. You might be thousands of miles away from family and friends, and depending on where you're studying, you might have to live without some creature comforts, like cereal for breakfast or your favorite pillow.

For some people, these challenges represent a great adventure. For others, they're frustrating and terrifying. Do extensive research, and hunt down other students who have been in the programs in the cities you're considering. Be sure to choose the best match for you, because a semester or a year is longer than you think.

30 *Contribute* to a school paper

If you plan on studying journalism or writing, or if you're passionate about a particular issue or subject, think about writing an article for your school paper. Even if you've never considered journalism, you can contribute a piece to the paper's op-ed section or pitch an article that applies to your specialty. It can feel gratifying to see people reading your name and your words. In the process you'll learn to work on a tight deadline, meet a specific word count, and express your thoughts effectively.

➤ HOW TO DO IT

If you want to write for the school paper on a regular basis, email someone at the paper to find out when the staff meets, and go to as many meetings as you can. You may have to do some grunt work before you get a byline, but if you have an idea, don't be afraid to pitch it in a meeting and see what happens. Eventually, you could start contributing regularly.

Let's say you have an idea for a story, but you're not interested in a long-term commitment. Nonreporters contribute to the op-ed sections of papers all the time, but to write a credible op-ed, you should be able to speak on the issue with some level of authority. What makes you the person for the job? Can you speak about the expansion of the engineering wing because you're an engineering student? Is the school population interested in your opinion on the new campus chapel because you're president of the atheists' club? If so, pitch your idea to the newspaper editor with your qualifications. But remember that editors are busy. If your pitch doesn't work the first time, try again.

The art of the pitch

A pitch, especially a cold one, should be cleanly written, intriguing, factual, convincing, and to the point. Here are two examples of pitches about a new baseball field opening on campus. If you were an editor, which would you choose?

* The old Green Towers baseball field would cost $5 million to renovate. The Hawks have been playing on the field for a long time. I love Green Towers and got my first home run there, actually. The field five miles away is nice, but it's not the same. The town says the new field has to be our new home because of tax reasons, but I think Green Towers should be our home field forever, and I should be the one to write about it in the school paper because I'm the third baseman.

* When our coach announced the Hawks would be leaving Green Towers baseball field next season in favor of a new home five miles away, I was heartbroken. I admit, the move makes sense. Green Towers' renovation would cost $5 million that the athletic commission doesn't have. The new field has space for a much-needed concession stand and more expansive bleachers. But that old, dilapidated field on campus carries centuries of historic victories and memories— ones that have shaped my experience as the Hawks' third baseman. Green Towers is deserving of a graceful farewell in the school paper, and I would be honored to write it.

Both pitches show strong opinions written by a firsthand expert. However, the second shows more research and clean writing ability. It is also a more compelling, passionate story. Go with number 2!!

31 Join an a cappella group

Fans of the TV series *Glee* know that there's almost nothing more fun than gathering some friends, composing tight harmonies, and performing in front of an audience. If you're a fan of musical performances, channel your inner songbird and join your school's a cappella group.

A cappella groups are basically crews of singers who adapt or write original music and present it without instruments. The vocal parts *become* the instruments. A cappella groups come in all shapes and sizes, from comedic to gospel to those that adapt pop or R&B songs. If they're good, they can be very, very impressive to watch.

Sure, some a cappella groups have a reputation for being corny. And sure, you may wonder how on earth you wound up onstage singing a medley of Madonna's greatest hits. But the corniness and camp are part of the fun, especially since you'll be with friends. Plus, while you're onstage having fun, you'll also be honing your singing, music theory, and theatrical skills.

➤ HOW TO DO IT

Depending on your university, there are probably at least a handful of a cappella groups you can join. Take your time and choose the right one for you. If you only want to sing soul, you probably don't want to join the barbershop quartet. Or, if you're dead serious about a cappella music, you might not want to join the group focused on making hilarious viral videos.

Once you've found your group, you may have to audition in front of a panel of current members. They'll probably want you to have

Finding your range

Maybe you're a great singer, but you've never classified your vocal range. Don't worry—it's easy to do. You will need a bit of music knowledge and a keyboard (or a keyboard app) to find it.

The scientific pitch notation key is designed to find out how high and how low you can comfortably sing. Use it to find out where you stand.

Soprano: C4 – A5

Mezzo-soprano: A3 – F5

Alto: F3 – D5

Tenor: B2 – D5

Baritone: G2 – E4

Bass: E2 – C4

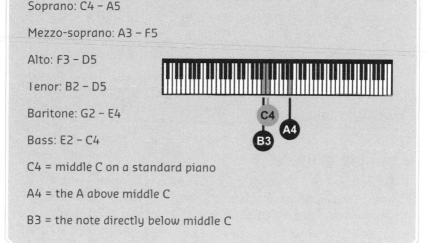

C4 = middle C on a standard piano

A4 = the A above middle C

B3 = the note directly below middle C

at least *some* singing and music-reading skills, or they might only be looking for a very particular vocal classification (soprano, tenor, alto, etc.). Choose an audition song you're comfortable with—one that easily falls into your vocal range—so the group can determine if you're a good fit.

As with any extra activity, make sure you're up for the commitment. Some groups participate in a cappella tournaments and have rehearsals several times a week. Others are loose and informal and only meet once in a while.

If you're *not* a singer but want to help with composition, why not contact the group and see if it could use another scribe? Wannabe singers are a dime a dozen, but good composers are a cappella holy grails.

THREE Taking Advantage of School

Make a web series about your school

T he ease with which almost anyone can create a YouTube series makes for a lot of junky stuff on the web. Cute cat videos and perfect marriage proposals are great, but why not create something meaningful or clever that speaks to your student body? Something that gets them engaged, talking, maybe even fired up about an issue. With little more than a smartphone or a webcam, some help from your talented friends, and an inspired idea, you can get everyone on campus talking. If you're interested in a film, acting, or editing career, this is a great chance to boost your portfolio.

➤ HOW TO DO IT

The hardest part of creating a web series can be coming up with an idea. You can enlist a few brains to help, but you're more likely to get people committed once you have a solid idea and a plan in place.

There's no secret to finding a perfect idea. Be observant on campus. See what people are talking about, and harness campus culture. Let inspiration find you. Maybe your school is missing some satire. May-

Funding?

If your idea is getting bigger and needs some dollars behind it, you can raise funds for your web series. The quickest, most direct approach is to use crowdfunding sites, like Kickstarter or Rock-etHub, where you can solicit both people you know and strangers. Some people have made millions for their projects that way!

be it needs an investigative reporter or a well-intended, perfectly legal hoax that proves a point. If executed correctly, any of these starting points could lead you somewhere great.

Unless you plan on doing the whole thing yourself, get your most brilliant friends on board to help you out. If it's a low-maintenance project, like sitting in front of a webcam every week and talking about what's been happening on campus, you'll want a few extra eyeballs to give you feedback. For a larger project, like a weekly drama series, take advantage of the talented student body and find qualified hands, like storyboarders, scriptwriters, actors, and directors. Of course, the smaller and cheaper the project, the easier it will be to sustain.

Once you've got one or two installments of your web series ready to go, create buzz through social media and flyer campaigns to whet students' appetite. Don't expect your video to catch fire the second it hits the airwaves. Give it time to spread around and generate interest. Encourage everyone you know to share, share, share. Send the video to any Facebook group or student club contact who might be interested. If it's a good video, it's bound to catch on.

33

Run for student government

If you're the go-getting type who wants to make real change on campus, consider running for student government. Not everyone at your school cares as much about administration transparency, equal rights, facilities problems, the arts, or *anything* as much as you do, so put that energy to good use and sign up for student government.

Being part of student government has many benefits. You'll be working side by side with the school administration, which will give you endless networking and learning opportunities. Your experience could pave the way for a career in management or politics. Most importantly, you'll be better equipped to make change on campus that you can be proud of for years to come.

➤ HOW TO DO IT

Here's how to run for student government.

1 / GET INVOLVED. Running for, and serving in, student government is no cakewalk, and it's not for everyone. To figure out if student government is for you, don't walk in blindly: Get involved. Attend student council meetings. Find out about structure, policies, campaign time lines, length of term, or any other details that might concern you.

2 / PREPARE TALKING POINTS. Besides the issues that interest you, find out which issues concern your fellow students. Maybe a lot of students are upset about dining hall prices or the lack of grassy areas on campus. Listening to what matters to them will help you find your talking points and show voters that you care about what they think.

It's a 24/7 job . . .

You may not be running for president of the United States, but you still need to keep your game face on if you're running for student government. In an age when almost everything gets blasted on the internet, remember to use common sense. Don't make insensitive comments or put yourself in compromising positions in public. You don't want anything you do, on or off the record, to negatively reflect on you and your campaign.

3 / SEND A MESSAGE. Draft a reasonable outline of your position as a candidate. Focus on two or three key points that directly affect a large portion of the student body. Don't make promises you can't keep. If this is your first time in student government, you'll need to learn the ins and outs before you can make major change.

4 / CAMPAIGN HARD. Promote yourself! Chat up your fellow students in classes or around campus. Post flyers and reach out using social media. Don't go on the offensive against your opponent at any stage of the campaign. It wouldn't reflect well on you, and your opponent might counterattack in the worst way. Just stick to your guns and be yourself, and you'll feel good about your campaign whether you win or not.

FOUR Being Social

34 *Host* a movie night in your dorm

I n all likelihood, you probably watch most movies and TV shows by yourself on your computer or smartphone. But wouldn't it be fun to host an official movie night or even a series of movie nights in your dorm? A movie night is about more than skipping the expensive movie theater; it's about gathering friends to share a fun, collective experience. Instead of heading out to yet another crowded frat party, your guests can show up in their pajamas, sit wherever they want, and just take it easy. Plus, at the end of the night, you don't even have to go anywhere. You're already home!

Dorm booze

Let's face it: People might want to drink on a movie night. Tempting as it may be to crack open a beer, dorms are not smart places to drink if you or your friends are underage. Resident advisors are obligated to write you up if they catch you drinking, and you're at risk of losing your housing. It's your dorm room and you set the rules, so if your friends insist on drinking, tell them to save the beer pong for the frat house. Tonight is about cinema!

➤ HOW TO DO IT

1 / Make sure your roommate or roommates are okay with you playing host to a movie night. The polite thing to do would be to invite them. Same goes for your neighboring floor mates, especially if you have thin walls.

2 / Once you've set a time and date, choose your movie. Pick one that your friends will enjoy, even if they've never seen or heard of it. Comedies and cult classics are great for movie nights because people can laugh, chat, and even rewind and replay their favorite scenes without missing too much plot. Save *Citizen Kane* for a quieter night.

Cool hunting

If you're struggling to come up with a fun, weird, seasonally appropriate movie selection, there's no shortage of ideas online. The A.V. Club's Inventory series, for instance, offers quirky rundowns on themed topics like "13 Good Performances in Bad Movies" and "Product Misplacement: 20 Brands Given Unhelpful Movie Associations," while their New Cult Canon series provides in-depth consideration of the movies that are still in the process of becoming cult hits. If you're looking for something a bit more artsy, or a bit more foreign, you might also look up some of the top ten lists at the Criterion Collection, where artists like Wes Anderson and James Franco select their ten favorite Criterion releases. And if you're still stumped after that, there's always good old Google. "Best worst monster movies of all time," anyone?

3 / Pitch your movie night to your friends as an epic night of movie-watching fun. Instead of breezily asking them to come over and share some screen time, send an invite that gets across how awesome the night will be.

"Are you ready . . . for KUNG FU?!

BAD DUBBING?!

And BRUCE. LEE'S. ABS?!!"

In the same invite, tell your friends what they need to bring: snacks, blankets, and pillows if you don't have enough.

4 / On the night of, provide plenty of popcorn and beverages of choice (maybe even a themed snack?), clear some space for everyone to sprawl out, and get the lighting situation just right.

If all goes well, maybe you can host another movie night the following month or convince your friends to rotate dorm rooms and movie curating. A movie-night series will give everyone something to look forward to each month.

35 *Throw* a dinner party

You don't have to go to an expensive restaurant to have a fancy dinner. You can host your very own *Downton Abbey*–worthy dinner party in the comfort of your dorm. You might not have candlelight, filet mignon, expensive red wine, fine china, loaded conversation, and a butler to clean it all up at the end, but you can still have a very proper (and very fun) dinner party with friends.

Chances are that you and your friends are more comfortable at the dining hall than at a sit-down dinner together, but that's what makes a dinner party fun. It's a chance to put on your Sunday (or your Friday) best, dust off the ol' table manners, and flex your culinary skills for a group of friends who will appreciate it.

➤ HOW TO DO IT

1 / Find a space to hold a dinner party, like the kitchen or a common area of your dorm that will be relatively quiet for the evening. You might need to reserve the space with your resident advisor, or you might need to do the cooking in the kitchen and then serve the dinner in your (comfortably cozy) dorm room. Another option is to ask a friend who has an apartment if you can use it for the evening (and invite the friend, of course).

2 / Draw up a tentative guest list and think of a few courses you'd be willing to cook for that number of people, perhaps with an enlisted helper or two. If you make the best mac and cheese on the planet, go for it. Maybe a friend prepares amazing brussels sprouts, or your roommate has always wanted to try making the perfect risotto. (See "Learn to Prepare One Meal Perfectly" for more prep tips.) If you

Lessons in etiquette

Because we're getting formal(ish) here, you may want to consult an expert on place settings. Here is how the late, great Emily Post suggests you set the table.

don't feel like cooking everything yourself, you can also make the evening a potluck.

3 / Once you've got a menu, send out an invitation via email. Or, better yet, handwrite one on high-quality cardstock. Ask friends to dress up, because . . . why not?

Remember that during a fancy dinner, ambience is everything. Dim mood lighting, candles (if your dorm allows them), and real place settings are a must. Even if you're using plastic cups, the napkins are stolen (ahem, *borrowed*) from the dining hall, and you had to turn your dorm desk into a dining table, you can still create an atmosphere of elegance that your friends will love.

FOUR Being Social

36 Prank your friends

Pranking your friends is probably the best down-time activity there is. If done well (and harmlessly), pranking can become a battle of wits among friends who want to one-up each other in ingenuity. Pranking should never be used for hazing or bullying (which you can be arrested for, FYI). Instead, it should be a creative game—one that has evolved way past shaving cream in the hand, writing on the face, and putting nasty stuff in peoples' food. After a good prank, you and your friends should be laughing, marveling at each other's ability to do such colossally stupid and incredibly creative stuff to each other.

➤ HOW TO DO IT

Before you prank, here are some ground rules.

- ➤ Don't be a bully. You only want to prank good friends who can take it and who are more than happy to dish it back. You should have a strong and equal friendship with the prankee. Inviting the whole floor to gang up on one person can be (very easily) misunderstood as cruel bullying, so try to keep your group of pranksters small and within your circle of trusted friends.

- ➤ Know your friend. Pranks are more successful when you capitalize on inside jokes, so try to think of something innocuous that your friend gets weirded out by, like balloons or creepy dolls, and start there. Never prey on someone's real fears or past traumas—that's just mean, not funny.

- ➤ Prepare for revenge. If you plan to prank, you ought to be able to handle retaliation.

- ➤ Get creative. You want to do something your friend won't expect.

The holy trinity of pranks

Here are three categories of pranks for any occasion.

1 / THE GROSS.

WHOM IT'S FOR: Your friend with the strongest stomach.

EXAMPLE: Switching salt out for sugar in the sugar packets at breakfast. That's some salty coffee!

2 / THE INCONVENIENT.

WHOM IT'S FOR: The friend who has a lot of free time.

EXAMPLE: Sticking colorful Post-it notes all over your friend's car, top to bottom, so the car looks painted in Post-its.

3 / THE HOAX.

WHOM IT'S FOR: The friend who doesn't mind being a little confused.

EXAMPLE: Inventing a conference or event that requires your friend to wake up at six in the morning and be somewhere. Extra points if you can get the friend to dress ridiculously.

37 _Start_ a dance party

Humankind has been dancing since the dawn of time. We've danced to appease the gods, to celebrate life, to seduce, to entertain, and to just relax. No one knows exactly why we're compelled to dance, but we do know that our brains are built to enjoy it.

There are so many kinds of parties in college, and whether or not it's written in the invitation, most benefit from a dance floor. Dancing brings out the best in people. Any trace of awkwardness is gone and forgotten once everyone is sweating, smiling, and dancing together like fools. Starting a dance party will liven up any get-together, and you don't have to know people that well to have a great time. Come to think of it, you don't have to _like_ anybody to have a good time, because when you're dancing, you don't have to talk at all. Booty shaking is the almighty peacemaking universal language of fun.

➤ HOW TO DO IT

Here's how to start a dance party.

1 / MAKE SURE IT'S OKAY WITH THE HOST. There's always a chance that neighbors have a tendency to complain about noise, or the crowd isn't right. Abide by your host's rules.

2 / CHECK ON THE MUSIC SITUATION. Who has the best music on her phone and won't mind manning the playlist for a while? (Maybe it's you!) Is there a decent sound system? What will it take to get the music just right?

3 / DESIGNATE A DANCE FLOOR. It should be somewhere spacious and highly visible, like in the middle of the room. If the dance vibe is right, it'll spread like a contagion. Soon, you'll have a raging dance party! Or at least a few of you will have fun, and in the end, that's all that matters.

4 / START DANCING. Once the music is set, go for it. Seriously. Just do it, even if you're not the best dancer in the world. How many times have you seen a horrible dancer having the time of his life? He might look as if he's embarrassing himself, but he's also having a ton of fun. Confidence is everything here.

5 / FIND OTHER DANCERS. Some people might look at you like you're crazy, but one or two will feel the vibe with you. You'll see them swaying, waiting to break out of their stationary shells. That's when you pounce and start dancing with them.

Creep alert!

Some people use dance parties as an excuse to get closer to you than you'd normally allow. You can usually tell who they are—they're dancing too close and care more about groping than the music. It can totally ruin a dance party if the vibe isn't right, so watch out for those creeps. And, just in case it's not already obvious, don't be a creep yourself either!

38 *Ask* someone on a date the old-fashioned way

Dating in the olden days meant a classy, polite courtship. At times it was *too* polite and restrictive, which is why many cultures have moved beyond the old courting. But in an age when it's so easy to meet someone at a party, make out, sext, rush into things, overcommit, and burn out on each other in a week, there is something kind of nice about asking someone on a real, formal date-date.

Asking someone on a date the old-fashioned way shows maturity, respect, and lots of guts. It takes more courage to ask someone to join you for dinner than it takes to text them the usual "What R U up 2?"

Your date might go so well that you'll never go back to party prowling.

➤ HOW TO DO IT

You know the feeling: you've gotten to know someone, you clearly feel chemistry between the two of you, and you'd like to take a shot at something more. When it feels appropriate, ask the person to have dinner or coffee, or go to a movie, or spend time bowling, or ice-skating, or something similarly innocent (and adorable). Asking face-to-face is a risk, but if you're confident and a little self-effacing about the whole "old-fashioned" thing, it might be a turn-on. However, if you're not ready to put someone on the spot like that, shoot them an email. Surely people in the olden days would have done the same if they had had the option.

If your date says yes, plan a fun evening out with the sole, explicit purpose of getting to know each other better. Keep the conversation

Rejected!

Almost everyone has been rejected at some point in their dating history. If your crush isn't down for a date, don't let it get to you. People have all kinds of reasons for saying no, and some of them might not have anything to do with you. As hard as a rejection may be to accept at first, don't spiral into a "NO ONE WILL DATE ME" hole. You'll get over the incident and move on, and it will make the next yes you get all the sweeter.

focused on common interests, making each other laugh, and being in the present—and keep sex and whatever dating agenda you may have off the table for now (though there's nothing wrong with a compliment or two). You may find that your date is even more amazing than you expected, or that he or she is actually kind of boring and you can't wait for the date to be over. Either way, maintain some old-fashioned precepts: Offer to pay for the check, since you issued the invitation, and end the evening with nothing more than a nice goodbye—and maybe a kiss. If the date went well, ask for another one! If it was a bust, oh well. At least you had a nice dinner!

39 *End* an argument

College is a new chapter in your life, and it's time to shed some old baggage. Maybe you have a standing feud with a high school friend, or a sibling rivalry, or a gripe with your folks. It can be freeing to forgive, forget, and move on. If you take the time to reevaluate the argument, you might find that you don't care about the initial grudge anymore. What was it? Your friend stole that crush whose name you can't even remember now? Or she said that nasty thing about you that one time? Or your brother never paid you back for something or other? Really, who cares? You've got better things to think about these days. Trying to patch things up shows maturity, and perhaps you'll restore some aspects of the old relationship.

➤ HOW TO DO IT

Put some thought into a phone call, email, or face-to-face conversation. Remember that the goal is to put things to rest, not to stir up old arguments by using the same approach you've used in the past. That approach didn't work before, and it probably won't work now. Instead, stay calm, and try not to hurl further blame. Focus on moving forward, not on the details of the problem. For example, "I know we've had some problems, but I hope we can move past them" is preferable to "I forgive you for owing me money." Even better, throw in an "I'm sorry" or two—even if it's hard.

If you can't help but revive the feud and you'd rather keel over and die than apologize, you're probably not ready to end the argument yet. In that case, savor the distance you've got right now, and just give it time.

Let go

You're over the grudge, and you've delivered the best Oscar winning "I forgive you" or "I'm sorry" speech ever written, and yet your friend, sibling, or rival *still* won't forgive and forget. Oh well. Let it go. Not everyone is willing to end a fight, or maybe the person is just not ready to wrap things up yet. Either way, you can feel closure just by knowing that you've taken the high road.

40 *Sever* toxic relationships

Just as some arguments need to be ended forever, some relationships are too toxic to keep up. You know the type: the overly needy friend who's never there for you when you need him, the person you're dating who's kind of controlling, the ex you keep going back to even though she doesn't love you and *always* makes you feel like crap. Everyone has been in these kinds of relationships, and rarely do they improve over time: The longer you stay in a toxic relationship, the more likely it is to escalate and mess with your life. You've got too much to do, and there are too many amazing people in the world to waste your time with drama. Cut 'em off, and breathe a little easier.

➤ HOW TO DO IT

How to go about severing a toxic relationship depends entirely on the situation and the relationship itself. If you're still in close contact and feel that the person will respond maturely to a straightforward rejection, gently deliver the news that it's over. If you've already attempted this approach and the person hasn't responded well and is still imposing on your life, make a real effort to ignore his or her phone calls, texts, Facebook posts, and emails, and maintain that same indifference when it comes to any face-to-face advances as well. The person should eventually get the hint that you're not interested in a friendship anymore. This approach requires an enormous exercise of will. You'll have to stand your ground to avoid sending mixed signals. If you feel like engaging, call or write to a good friend instead. Or, go for a run. Anything else.

Just a bad friend, or an abusive friend?

Here are some of the signs of abusive relationships:

* The person constantly keeps tabs on you.

* You feel like you're losing your mind over the relationship.

* The person makes you feel like everything is your fault, or turns all his or her questionable deeds around on you.

* You're constantly bending over backward to please the person while devaluing your own thoughts and beliefs.

* There are insane ups and downs, from explosive verbal abuse to pleading apologies.

If you've been the victim of abuse, visit your school's psychological services department for help, or go to the National Domestic Violence Hotline at hotline.org, which addresses many forms of abuse and offers professional, confidential guidance by phone.

If these approaches don't work, and you're beginning to sense that you're in danger from a former friend, consult campus police. The situation may not get to that point, and all you'll need to do is give the relationship some distance, but it's good to be aware of potential danger, just in case.

41 *Hold* a karaoke night

ne of the best inventions to hail from Japan—besides Playstation and karate, of course—is karaoke. Karaoke, which means "empty orchestra," is an interactive program where a person, or group of people, sings along to a song's score while reading the lyrics on a screen . . . usually at top volume. It's a fun, cheesy, and entertaining activity, and if you're an accomplished singer or a veritable showman, it's a great chance to show off.

While doing karaoke alone in your room can be a blast, the best kind of karaoke is usually with a group of friends. Karaoke can transform the shyest of classmates into the next Beyoncé, or you might find your most theatrical, over-the-top friends are dreadful singers. Karaoke can be full of surprises.

➤ HOW TO DO IT

You can do karaoke in your dorm room or apartment by using cheap karaoke computer software, your computer speakers, and a microphone; by purchasing a cheap karaoke machine with limited functionality; or by simply looking up YouTube videos of karaoke versions of your favorite songs.

You can also go out to a bar or club. A lot of bars host karaoke and have impressive song banks to choose from. These bars usually host their own karaoke nights on a weekly or monthly basis, so you'll have to do some research and stay on top of schedules before you head out. However, twenty-one-plus rules usually apply for entry, unless the venue is hosting a special all-ages, alcohol-free night.

Another option for on-the-town karaoke is to go to a karaoke venue with private rooms. These rooms usually charge by the hour, so if you

can pack in a lot of friends, the cost per person will be cheaper. Private rooms are also great because you don't have to fight with other patrons to get on the mic, and you don't have to worry about singing in front of strangers. Renting a private room is a really great birthday party option, but let's be serious—karaoke never goes out of style (in part because it's never really *in* style either).

Love hosting a lot?

Many venues with a karaoke night pay freelance hosts to stay on top of the song order, rally enthusiasm, and even sing a song or two to get the crowd warmed up. Karaoke hosting is a low-commitment way to make a little extra money, and if you're a die-hard karaoke fan, you'll have a ton of fun in the process. Ask your favorite karaoke venue if it's in need of a karaoke host, and see what happens.

42 *Take* a road trip

You and your friends have been living in the same college town, eating the same dining hall food, and studying hard in the same old library for months. Isn't it time to get away?

The idea of taking a road trip may conjure visions of an overwhelming, far-flung, ill-fated adventure. You know the script to those road-trip horror movies: The car falls in a ditch, the friends hitchhike with dangerous characters, they wind up lost in a remote, *Deliverance*-esque town, and it all culminates in a bear fight, a few murders, and deepened friendships. Right?

Not really. In real life, you have the power to control your own road trip. You can plan each and every minute in advance if you want to and ensure that you have all the amenities you crave—including continuous cell phone service. You can choose your own difficulty level along with your adventure. So give it a shot. A road trip is a great bonding activity and a great way to relax and get away for a while.

➤ HOW TO DO IT

You may only have a weekend, or you may have an entire month. You may have access to a car already, or you may have to rent one. You may want to do a sightseeing tour and jump back and forth between motels and campgrounds, or you may want to drive to a beach, rent a house for a week, and not move a muscle. There's no wrong way to go road tripping.

Before you hit the road, figure out the destination(s), accommodation requirements, route, time, budget, friend-invite list, and, most importantly, music. You do not want to be crammed in a car for hours

and hours without some solid listening material, whether it's an open-road playlist, a podcast you love, or an audiobook that everyone's excited about "reading."

Stay reasonable and flexible, because on any kind of trip (and especially a road trip) you're bound to encounter unpredictable factors like inclement weather, map failure, or just plain exhaustion.

Once you've got all the details sorted out, the open road is yours. Until you're tired of it and want to head back home, that is.

Can I get a lifeline?

Leaving campus and heading out into the world comes with some safety risks. One way to feel safe is to have lifelines connecting you to your home base. Before you head out, give several people (your parents, other friends) copies of your trip route and schedule. If you have cell reception, check in with them every day. You can even take checking in a step further and allow them to trace your location through an app like Find My Friends. A bit of prep will be worth a lot of peace of mind.

43 Go above and beyond for a friend's birthday

Birthday celebrations can fall into a rut, albeit a festive rut. The typical formula: You go to a restaurant, park, or apartment, give your friend nice gifts, sing "Happy Birthday to You," and have a great time. But how about doing something a little extra? Giving your friend *any* gift or throwing him *any* party feels nice, but doing something that takes a little more effort, creativity, and thought feels even better. Shaking up the typical birthday party formula doesn't have to cost a ton of money or take up all your time, but it could make your friend's birthday his best ever. Unless your friend is made of stone, he will probably feel ridiculously special.

➤ HOW TO DO IT

You can plan a party or gathering, or you can give an awesome, personalized gift. Either way, focus on what you know about your friend. Think back on conversations you've had, and get creative. Nothing is impossible—but some things might be more expensive than others. So figure out a budget and stick to it. If you have an incredible idea but it will cost a bit more, consider pooling money from other partygoers or friends and making your plan a joint effort.

For the quiet types . . .

The ideas below all assume that your friend appreciates the loud and outrageous. Honestly, cooking your friend a meal he loves or paying for a much-needed night out at the movies is already going above and beyond the call of birthday duty. No matter what you do for your friend, the point is to do or give them something personal that shows you've been paying attention to who they are and what they like.

Here are some examples of how to turn a friend's likes into birthday gold.

➤ Has your friend always wanted to go on a ferry ride? Take her on one . . . and have her friends waiting onboard to surprise her with cake!

➤ Do you and your friend have a recurring inside joke about a unicorn showing up to his party? Call your crafty collaborators, sew some white fabric and "mane" yarn together, roll up a horn out of cardboard, draw some eyeballs, and, voilá! You've made a raggedy version of a unicorn costume. Someone needs to wear this work of art, and it ought to be you.

➤ Did your friend have to miss a recent concert and is still extremely bummed about it? There are two things you can do: Get everyone to pitch in for tickets to the artist's next show, or get all her friends to dress up as the musician she missed. Surprise!

44 *Show* some love

Chances are that you love somebody. Whether it's your dad, your little sister, your friend, or your significant other, you love someone close to you—but you have trouble saying it.

Telling people you love them isn't easy, unless it's already a habit (like when you say "Love ya!" at the end of a phone conversation with your mom). If it's a new thing, saying, "I love you" can make you feel vulnerable and silly. But it's the truth, isn't it? And when you say it in a noncreepy, appropriate, genuine way, you'll pave the way for an even closer relationship.

The bottom line: "I love you" just feels *good* to *say.*

➤ HOW TO DO IT

Here are different kinds of "I love yous" and how to use them.

➤ "I love you, man" or "I love you guys!" For friends. Works well in emails, during moments of celebration, or when you just can't help it.

➤ "I love you, [family member]." If you don't say it very often, this might be a very emotional moment. Prepare to follow it up with something like, "Seriously, you've always been there for me, and I don't say it enough."

➤ "I'm falling in love with you." For someone you've been dating for a while. In relationships, the L-bomb moves everything to a whole new level, so you're taking a deliberate risk here. If you've only gone on a couple of dates, save the declaration of love for later. Saying, "I love you" can be very awkward if the other person isn't ready to say it back.

➤ "You're my friend, but I'm *in* love with you." Approach with caution. Dropping the L-word into a friendship is a very risky move. It *might* work, but if you both have feelings for each other, the relationship should probably move organically, not by the sudden unleashing of an L-bomb. You run the risk of losing a friend if you make this move, but if you just can't keep it inside, be bold! This could change everything.

➤ "You don't know me, but I love you." Never do this. Nope. Forget it.

Welcome to breakup city

If your significant other doesn't feel the same way you do, it might be time to break up. Breakups can be one of the hardest things in the world; here you are putting your heart on the table, and there it is, getting stomped on. No matter how you feel about the breakup, you should always respect the other person's feelings and mourn the relationship in private or with a few close friends. And don't use your breakup as fuel to beat yourself up or feel unlovable. You *will* get through it over time—you just need to feel crappy for a while.

FIVE Body and Health

45 Get a physical for no serious reason

After our childhood vaccinations and checkups, and before our elderly years call for regular visits to the doctor, most of us don't see a doctor often unless something's wrong. But going to the doctor for an annual checkup is important for adults, too! While you probably don't need to be paranoid about health issues, it's better to be informed about your health—things like your cholesterol, blood pressure, or BMI (body mass index)— than be left to wonder.

As a college student, you probably have access to a doctor right on campus who would be happy to see you for a physical. Most of the time, on-campus student health services are quite low cost, so you might as well get checked out while you're a student.

➤ HOW TO DO IT

During a typical physical, your doctor will check your height, weight, and vitals. He or she may also test your reflexes, examine your ears and sinuses, and look for any abnormalities on your skin or in your throat. Women should also have annual pelvic and breast exams, and men should get prostate and testicular exams as they age.

Some blood or lab work—like cholesterol tests, AIDS tests, or urinalysis—isn't automatically part of a doctor's physical exam procedure, so you may have to request it. Ask if the doctor recommends any specific tests based on your medical history.

Cholesterol, WTF?

Cholesterol is a waxy fat substance that usually helps keep your body balanced and working properly. When your cholesterol is too high, however, it sticks to your arteries and causes health risks. If you have high cholesterol, your doctor might prescribe some meds and an overhaul of your health regimen to bring it back down to a healthy level. To lower your cholesterol, you can also cut back on trans fats (which exist in certain store-bought foods like cookies) and saturated fats (found in some dairy products and certain kinds of cooking oils) and replace them with heart-healthy food. This is a smart choice whether or not you have high cholesterol.

Here are four kinds of foods the Mayo Clinic recommends eating to help lower your cholesterol:

* Oatmeal, oat bran, and high-fiber foods

* Fish and omega-3 fatty acids

* Walnuts, almonds, and other nuts

* Olive oil

46 Go rock climbing

Rock climbing is one of the most glorious ways you can exercise. More than a full-body workout, rock climbing is an exercise of wits, a triumph over fear, a literal balancing act, and a chance to see the world from new heights. If you're sick of the same old jogging routine and want to try something new, rock climbing is a gratifying and completely different type of challenge. Even if you've never been rock climbing before, you can find safe and relatively easy programs for beginners.

➤ HOW TO DO IT

If you're a total beginner, find someone knowledgeable and experienced to help you out. Only a professional instructor can teach you the moves, provide the proper equipment (and show you how to use it), and prevent you from getting hurt. Safety when rock climbing is serious business (it's a long way down) so make sure you trust the person who's training you.

Do some research on rock-climbing gyms or facilities in your area. If you're in a more rural area and the weather's sunny, you might have access to outdoor rock climbing. In more metropolitan areas, there are indoor facilities with artificial rock walls usable year-round.

Fear of heights?

A fear of heights is completely natural, but unless you have a serious phobia, there are ways to power through it for your first rock climb. If you're afraid of heights, get to know the ins and outs of the security equipment and ask the instructor lots of questions before you climb. Sometimes a little assurance is all you need. Remember that the more you do it, the more comfortable you'll become.

As a beginner, you will probably do top-rope climbing, which means that one end of the rope is anchored at the top of the climb and the other end is attached to a belayer—the instructor—who will prevent you from falling. You may also do simple bouldering, which involves ropeless climbs on small boulders low to the ground. Rock-climbing facilities usually offer private lessons, group rates, and even certification classes if you're looking to take rock climbing to the next level.

47 *Improve* Your Diet

One of the biggest enemies to a healthy weight can be carbohydrates. Carbs are everywhere, especially in foods like breads, cereals, cookies, potato chips, alcohol, and starches. Surprisingly, carbs can end up causing more fat to build up on your body than fats can. Complex carbohydrates convert very quickly into blood glucose, and the body can only store so much of it before it piles up as body fat. By carbo-loading, you're basically junking up your body rather than nurturing it.

If you replace half of your carb intake with vegetables, dairy products, nuts (if you can eat them), seafood, and meat (if you eat it), you'll be doing your body a huge favor.

It's not easy to cut down on carbs, since they're everywhere and tend to be easy to buy (and supertasty!). It's simpler, for example, to pop into a bagel shop while running an errand than to hunt down fresh salad ingredients. Yes, you might have to cook more and be choosier about the places where you eat, but halving your carb intake will lead to higher energy, healthy weight loss, and much better eating habits in the long run.

➤ HOW TO DO IT

Assess what your options are for cutting carbs. Does your dining hall offer low-carb meals? Are there nearby health food stores you can try? Can you easily substitute a salad, omelet, or steak for a sandwich and chips? If the answer is yes, you're in a good position to cut down on less nutritious food.

Beware the fad diets

Some of-the-moment diets and weight-loss products work, but if something sounds too good to be true, it probably is. There is no miracle weight-loss drug, and it's not a good idea to do drastic things, like limit your diet to one food item. These fad diets are not sustainable, and you'll only gain the weight right back. Plus, they can be incredibly damaging to your health. Steer clear of fad diets and run any new diet regimen you want to try by your doctor. As with most things, a healthy diet requires balance, not extremes.

Once you get into the habit of going for healthier options, you'll start feeling better and will probably drop a few pounds—but keeping it up is tough. If you slip up a couple of times and binge on carb-heavy foods, don't freak out. And don't give up entirely! Halving your carbs is a great goal, but sneaking a cookie or two won't kill you.

48 Give your eyes a computer break

Between researching and writing papers, catching up with friends on Facebook or via email, and playing games or watching funny videos, you probably spend a good amount of time in front of a computer screen. Unfortunately, our eyes haven't adapted to staring at these glaring, reflective screens for long periods of time. Over the course of a few years, the strain can deteriorate your overall eye health. There's even a name for it: computer vision syndrome. If you've got it, you may experience eyestrain, headaches, dry eyes, deteriorating distance vision, or any number of vision issues.

The good news? Some of these problems can be rectified, and better yet, they can be avoided altogether. Sure, eye health isn't a very exciting topic—it's right up there with preventing carpal tunnel syndrome—but in the long run, your eye function is probably one of the most important things you should be taking care of.

➤ HOW TO DO IT

The American Optometric Association recommends these steps for avoiding computer vision syndrome.

1 / REDUCE GLARE. Minimize glare by turning your screen away from overhead lighting or sunlight. If you can't get around the glare, buy an antiglare screen filter.

2 / ADJUST THE SCREEN LOCATION. The screen should be four or five inches below your eye level, with the center being twenty to twenty-eight inches from your eyes.

Head, shoulders, knees, and toes

Your eyes aren't the only body parts affected when you've been sitting at a computer for hours. Your back, shoulders, and neck can suffer, too. To avoid extra strain, adjust your chair height so that your feet are flat on the floor when you're working at your computer. Your chair should be comfortable, and if it has arms, you should adjust them so that they support your arms, taking the pressure off your wrists.

3 / TAKE BREAKS. Rest your eyes for fifteen minutes every two hours, and focus on something in the distance for twenty seconds every twenty minutes. This will help your eyes refocus and help prevent strain.

4 / BLINK! Blink frequently to avoid dry eye.

5 / VISIT AN EYE DOCTOR. Get regular eye exams and track your progress. An eye doctor may be able to help you avoid further deterioration or even help you heal the problems you've already developed from computer vision syndrome. Besides, eye exams can be kind of cool and colorful.

49

Speak up
about dining hall woes

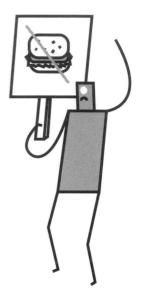

When you eat in your school dining hall, do you have to ask yourself whether you just saw a mouse? Do you wonder why the chef isn't wearing any gloves while mixing the tuna salad? Do you have to hunt high and low for any vegetarian or vegan options? Are you forced to dodge falling objects (tiles, fans) from the ceiling? If so, it might be time to speak up.

The dining hall is a huge part of your life at college. Unless you plan to eat peanut butter sandwiches in your dorm room every day, part of each day will be spent within those walls. Your status as a student makes you a paying customer in the establishment, and to a reasonable extent, you should feel you're being treated like one. Food, facilities, staff, sanitation—all should be up to par. But, as in any restaurant, issues can come up. Maybe the school didn't take into account the large Islamic population at your university, and the dining hall needs to offer an alternative to pork dinners. Or the prices are too exorbitant for most students. Or, despite complaints, there's *still a freaking mouse problem*!

If you feel there's a serious issue (or maybe a few) in your dining hall, why not tell someone? Change won't happen unless somebody speaks up. If your request is attended to, you'll be doing the whole student body a favor.

Making the most of it

While you wait for change to come, you can liven up your unappetizing, unhealthy dining hall food. Add spices or health supplements like probiotics, or keep a stash of fresh produce in your dorm to mix with the greasy meat-and-carb dining hall smorgasbord. DIY gourmet dining!

➤ HOW TO DO IT

Okay, let's not go overboard. This is a university dining hall, not a five-star restaurant. If you keep your demands reasonable and you have enough evidence to support your claim, the school is likely at least to consider your request.

1 / GATHER EVIDENCE. If you can, take plenty of photos of the problem areas.

2 / GAIN SUPPORT. At the end of the day, dining halls are a business. They need to know that *many* students want change, not just one. You'll want the support of fellow students behind you, so talk to them. Gather signatures, numbers, and testimonials to prove that this is a issue for many students, and that the school should listen up.

3 / INFORM FACILITIES. Make an appointment with the school office that runs the dining hall. Show your evidence and support to the department head. Be cool, collected, and polite when you present your grievances.

4 / TELL THE STUDENT BODY. If you've met with the dining hall office a dozen times and there are still no changes, go to the student government. Spread the word. Take your cause to social media. Fuel passion. If all else fails, you could hit 'em where it hurts and organize a boycott. If you end up organizing with other students, remember your original goal: change in the dining hall. Once you get what you want or come to a compromise, graciously end the war and chow down on whatever it was you wanted so badly.

50 *Learn* self-defense

Hopefully, you'll never be in a situation where you have to use any self-defense skills. But whether you're in an urban area or a suburban one, and whether you're six-foot-five or five-foot-nothing, you can gain confidence and a little peace of mind by taking a self-defense class.

Self-defense classes will teach you a thing or two (or three) about protecting yourself in dangerous situations. You'll learn how to avoid dangerous situations in the first place, how to make defensive moves that an attacker might not expect, and how to use smarts, not just strength, to get out of a tight spot.

Self-defense skills can't get you out of every dangerous situation. But you'll be more prepared if something *does* happen after you've practiced escaping from unsafe scenarios over and over again with an expert. Plus, the confidence you'll gain from learning self-defense will help you walk the streets with your head held a little higher.

➤ HOW TO DO IT

Some self-defense classes focus more on martial arts, and some focus solely on how to escape from an attacker. Before you sign up, read the class description to make sure it's right for you.

Whatever kind of self-defense class you take, you will probably learn things like how, when, and where to strike an attacker; how to escape from holds; and what to do if you're on the ground. One popular self-defense martial art is an Israeli method called krav maga—meaning "contact combat"—which teaches students how to defend themselves in hand-to-hand combat. It can be physically

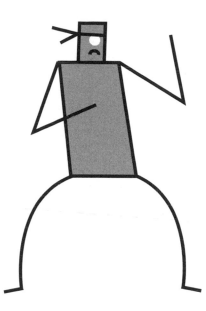

grueling, but self-defense usually is!

Your school may offer free self-defense classes as part of the curriculum, so check the course offerings to see if you can learn some self-defense and get credit for it. You can also search for gyms or community centers that offer self-defense classes.

Get street smart

When it comes to safety, common sense is your first defense. Here are some valuable, simple tips for handling a potentially threatening situation—without using your fists at all!

* Have your keys readily available in your pocket so you don't have to fumble for them in your bag.

* Avoid texting, emailing, etc., while walking, given the cell-phone-theft rate and chance of being mugged in the process. In other words, don't be distracted.

* Walk with a hand in your pocket. You'll give the impression that you might be carrying something to defend yourself with.

* Carry something useful on your keychain, like a flashlight or a whistle or another object that makes noise. If you carry pepper spray, practice using it before you get into a dangerous situation.

51 *Learn* to pick your produce

Everyone knows that fresh fruits and vegetables are good for you. Yet choosing the ripest, most nutrient-rich, quality fruits and vegetables isn't something they teach in school. Unless you grew up on a farm or your family put effort into bestowing upon you a superior knowledge of produce, you might not know how to pick the best fruits and vegetables from the shelf.

Why should you care? First and foremost, buying your own produce will you save money: For the price of that $10 salad at a café, you could have bought *pounds* of the same ingredients. Second, buying your own produce will ensure that you have something healthy to snack on when the dining hall is closed, rather than chomping down vending machine potato chips. And most importantly, by buying your own produce, you get to exercise quality control. Some restaurants don't use fresh produce or wash it properly, which means it won't taste as good and it could very well make you sick. If you learn to pick your own produce, you'll know you're getting the best stuff.

➤ HOW TO DO IT

Start by finding a reliable source—a store that values freshness and quality. Farmers' markets and stores that sell local produce are great, because the food probably hasn't been damaged by shipping or kept in cold storage. But many grocery stores sell perfectly good produce; you just have to do a little research. Ask around, look at online reviews, and be smart. If a store is generally filthy and other food is past its sell-by date, it's no place for produce.

Veggie upkeep

Keeping your chosen produce fresh and tasty is a whole different challenge. Some items, like carrots, keep for a long time if refrigerated. Others, like snow peas, should be eaten as soon as possible. If you cut or peel anything that you're not going to use, wrap it up and stick it in the fridge immediately. Keep produce separate from meat, and always rinse it thoroughly before eating.

Once you find your spot, follow these simple tips for picking the good stuff.

For fruits

> Avoid fruits with soft spots, bruises, or off coloring.

> Avoid citrus fruits that are too firm; they are probably dried out.

> Look for fruits with a light, sweet aroma, and avoid those with a pungent, syrupy odor.

For veggies

> Most leafy greens should be evenly colored and unbroken.

> Avoid potatoes, onions, and other root vegetables with cracks.

> Avoid anything that smells bad.

And if you're not sure quite how to pick out the best item in a given bunch, go ahead and ask someone in the store to provide some guidance! They're usually more than happy to help.

52 *Get* support

College can be an emotionally and psychologically challenging time. Your entire world is changing, you're making big decisions about the rest of your life, you're moving into a new phase of adulthood—it's a lot to handle. If you're undergoing something difficult psychologically, you're probably not alone.

The great thing about many colleges is that students have easy access to mental health services. In many cases, these services are part of the tuition benefits and are located right on campus. With some research, you'll probably find accredited psychologists on site as well as support groups, access to referrals, and more. It's not always easy to find this wealth of support once you leave campus life behind, so you may as well take advantage of the helping hands around you while you're still in school.

➤ HOW TO DO IT

1 / As clichéd as it may sound, the first step is to accept that you need help. Everyone, at one point or another, deserves a supportive boost, whether it's due to mild anxiety or something much more serious.

2 / Go to the student health services center and tell a doctor what you're going through. The doctor can refer you to the proper professional, on or off campus, or recommend a support group.

Finding mental health treatment can be a lot like dating: you may not find the right therapist or group immediately, and you may have to shop around a bit. Don't write off therapy just because you had one less-than-ideal experience. Your mental health is a long-term commitment, and patience will get you results.

Shrink breakdown

Here's a basic description of the most common types of psychological treatments:

* Psychoanalysis: A treatment in which you and a professional map out your innermost subconscious thoughts and work to shed unhelpful ways of thinking. Psychoanalysis can be rigorous and entail a high commitment.

* Group psychotherapy: A professional guides a group of people experiencing a similar issue, ranging from anger management to eating disorders to alcoholism to anxiety.

* Cognitive psychotherapy: This one-on-one treatment is aimed at defeating unproductive or damaging cycles of thinking.

* Behavioral psychotherapy: Also a type of one-one-one therapy, it focuses on changing immediate behaviors, such as phobias or alcoholism, without digging deep into your history.

* Psychiatry: In addition to providing therapeutic treatment, psychiatrists are generally licensed to prescribe medication and conduct physical exams.

* Expressive therapy: This therapy uses creativity to heal wounds. Art, dance, drama, music, and writing are standard outlets in expressive therapy.

53

Get smart about substances

Your parents, your teachers, and McGruff the Crime Dog have probably all taught you about the dangers of drugs and alcohol. While it's true that drugs and alcohol can be dangerous, it's also true that many college students want to experiment with these substances. And if you *are* going to try something new, it's helpful to be informed.

Perhaps the only message you've heard about drugs and alcohol is "Don't do it," but knowing what you're getting into, how to use substances in moderation, and how to handle potentially dangerous situations is essential. Being uninformed can lead to alcohol poisoning, overdose, addiction, arrest, or just public embarrassment—all the things you've been warned about. Getting informed about drugs and alcohol will give you at least a degree of control over your substance use.

Also, be aware: The laws about drinking and drugs can vary from state, so make sure you know the laws and understand the risks before indulging.

➤ HOW TO DO IT

Lots of standard scientific literature is free online, like on the National Institute on Drug Abuse website. Your doctor will also be able to tell you how your body will react to drugs and alcohol and what the effects of certain doses are likely to be.

A good rule of thumb is, if you're doing a drug or drinking for the first time, go slow and have someone experienced (and sober) monitor your intake and look out for you. Make sure you're in a safe envi-

Avoiding a hangover

The best way to avoid a hangover is not to drink too much in the first place, but here are some remedies that may help you avoid a crippling headache (and mountains of regret) in the morning:

* Eat a full meal before you drink.

* Drink a glass of water between each alcoholic drink, then about two eight ounce glasses of water before you go to bed.

* Take an ibuprofen pill before you fall asleep.

ronment with people you trust, and obviously don't drive under the influence of any substance.

A fun way to learn about drinking is to gain a respect for the pastime, rather than binge drinking at a frat party (a terrible and dangerous idea on so many levels). You could become something of a cocktail expert by learning to appreciate the subtle taste, prep, and mixology of fancy drinks. Mixing cocktails lets you make alcohol do your bidding, rather than letting it get the better of you. Plus, it's a cool party trick.

However, there is no perfect formula to avoid overdoing it, and people can overdose or become addicted no matter how much they learn about substances. Being informed, realistic with yourself, and respectful toward your body are all steps toward avoiding major problems that can affect your whole life.

Of course, if you feel that you or someone you know has a problem with drugs or alcohol, visit the student health services center and ask about substance counseling.

54 *Get* even smarter about safe sex

Knowledge is more than power when it comes to safe sex—it can potentially save your life. You probably learned about safe sex in high school, but it doesn't hurt to brush up on the finer points. The mantra "Always use a condom" has been drilled into your head by now, but it's easy to use poor judgment when in the heat of the moment or in a semicomfortable relationship. If you approach sex with your eyes closed and throw caution to the wind, you're risking grave consequences, from gonorrhea to pregnancy to death. Putting in a little effort to refresh your memory and learn new things about safe sex (there's *always* more to learn!) will keep staying safe in the forefront of your mind.

➤ HOW TO DO IT

Frequent medical checkups and STI (sexually transmitted infection) tests are crucial. Women should get an annual ob-gyn exam (including a Pap smear at age 21), and everyone who is sexually active should be tested when a risk or a new partner is introduced (even if you've worn a condom!). Be sure to ask for specific tests if you have specific concerns, because some diseases, like herpes, are not always included in the standard STI test regimen.

On your own, you can find out all about STIs through sources like the U.S. Centers for Disease Control and Prevention and the American Sexual Health Association, or at websites like Womenshealth.gov, CDC.gov, and ASHASexualHealth.org. There's a lot of misinformation about sex and STIs online, so find a few reliable sites and check them regularly for updates and new information.

One of the most important things you can do to stay sexually healthy and safe is to be open and honest, and to encourage openness and honesty in your partners. Never let shame keep you from telling someone that you have an STI. And *always* use protection, no matter what your new partner tells you. Better safe than . . . well, you know the rest.

The grim reality . . .

You may not know some of these important facts about STIs.

* Human papilloma virus, or HPV, is one of the most insidious—yet least discussed—epidemics on the planet. It's so common that it affects 50 percent of sexually active people at some point in their lives and a whopping *80 percent* of women. It often goes undiagnosed and can lead to long-term problems, like genital warts and cervical cancer. Testing for women exists but is not currently recommended for men, and condoms are not necessarily an effective prevention method, as the virus can be passed from skin-to-skin contact. Vaccines are, however, available to prevent certain strains of HPV.

* There are now HIV treatments that enable patients to live healthy lives despite the disease, but they can be very expensive—around $23,000 a year. That's a hefty chunk of change to pay for the rest of your life.

* If you get cold sores, you can spread genital herpes to your partners through oral contact. Dental dams are a good preventative measure, but it's best not to engage in oral sex at all during an outbreak.

55 *Enlist* a workout buddy

Finding the motivation to start a new workout routine can be tough. Most days, your warm, cozy bed is so much more inviting than a cold, stinky gym. If only you had a drill sergeant to wake you up and force you to put on your sneakers!

Well, you probably can't get a drill sergeant, but you *can* get the next best thing: a friend. If you're the type who needs a nudge to get moving, enlist a friend or two to start working out with you on a regular basis. It's also a great way to bond with the people you already know you like.

➤ HOW TO DO IT

How you enlist a workout buddy depends on your friends, your preferences, and your workout. Some people absolutely hate jogging with someone else; others wouldn't dream of running alone. Some people want to attend yoga classes with friends; others want to go solo. Talk to your friends about their exercise interests and find the buddy whose workout wants match your own.

Although having a workout buddy is a good way to stay motivated, you shouldn't become 100 percent dependent on your buddy to get you moving. Schedules shift, people lose steam, and things change. Treat your workout partnership as an experiment at first, and if it becomes a regular thing, great! If not, have a backup plan, even if it means setting twelve alarms to wake you up.

Team sports

Here are some two-person workouts you can pitch to your friend:

★ Frisbee

★ Tennis

★ Weight lifting with a spotter

★ Boxing

★ One-on-one basketball

★ Badminton

★ Volleyball

SIX Spoil Yourself

56 *Change* your hair

Your hair is like this magical element growing out of your scalp that can completely transform your appearance. It's easy to get comfortable with one style and assume that absolutely nothing else will look good on you, but comfortable can get kind of boring after a while. And anyway, "just because" isn't a very good reason to do anything: It's not a good enough reason to keep your hairstyle, and it's *definitely* not a good reason to get a tattoo or legally change your name to This Guy. So if you're feeling bored with your look, own it! That sense of boredom can provide the inspiration you need to change your hairstyle. (Other great reasons to overhaul your coif include breakups, career shifts, birthdays, and other major life transitions.) When you make a major change to your hair, the worst-case scenario is that you don't love your new style and you change it again.

➤ HOW TO DO IT

You know those people with interesting, offbeat, or superclean haircuts you've always admired but never thought you could pull off? You could be dead wrong.

Think of your favorite style ideas, and gather some inspirational images to show a hairstylist. Don't limit the styles, even if you think a look might not work on your hair. Your stylist can tell

Product is magic

If you're looking for a short-term change and want something different for, say, a night out with friends, hair product is your ultimate accessory. With product, you can create dreads, add texture to fine hair, straighten out wavy hair, and more—and wash it all out when you're done.

you more about what will work and what won't, based on your hair type, bone structure, and complexion. He or she can also combine a few different inspirations into a unique style that works for you. Be open to suggestion from your stylist, but don't cave in and say you're satisfied with a style that you don't really like. After all, *you're* the one who will be walking around with that hairstyle, not your stylist! If standing up for your opinions is difficult for you, bring a highly opinionated friend to help offer some additional critique.

When choosing a salon or barber shop, look for stylists who specialize in the style you're going for. Some places are strictly for men, some for women, some for simple assembly-line 'dos, some for coloring, and some for braiding. Don't spend your money unless you feel confident and at ease in a place.

57 *Fill out* your wardrobe

T hrift stores are the best. Okay, not every item in every thrift store is the best—thrift stores are also home to strange '70s pantsuits, muumuus, and some of the creepiest curios you'll ever find. But if you dig deep enough, you can discover some treasures and spend a lot less than at a regular retail store.

For decades, people have been picking up excellent work clothes, pants, dresses, scarves, jackets, shoes, and even kitchenware from thrift stores. You can find plenty of lightly worn items in fabulous shape. Seriously, where else can you walk away with five awesome pairs of pants in your size for $20?

If you're missing some key items in your wardrobe or just want some cool new shorts or sweaters, it's time to treat yourself. Spend an afternoon at a local Goodwill, Salvation Army, or other thrift store—and go nuts.

Sell your own!

You might be able to sell your own clothes at local thrift or consignment stores (but not at donation-based stores like Goodwill). Find out which stores buy clothes from the public. You'll have better luck selling clothes that are in season, like sweaters in late fall and sandals in spring. Also, scope out the store's style—for instance, '80s fashions or '50s vintage—and only bring clothes that fit the aesthetic. And *always* wash, iron, and fold the clothes beforehand. Good luck!

➤ HOW TO DO IT

Goodwill and the Salvation Army are the most common chain thrift stores, and there's probably one near you. Smaller, privately owned stores might use the word *vintage* or *consignment* instead of *thrift* or *charity* in their names. Vintage and consignment shops sell clothing that's usually been more carefully selected than what you'll find at a larger, chain thrift store, but they can also be much more expensive.

At a large thrift store, you'll find seemingly endless rows of clothes—and you might have to dig deep to pull out the gems. Thrift shopping is more of a time investment than a money investment, but if you take the time to go through the racks, it'll definitely be worth it.

Always try on clothing before you buy it, and check for damage. If you find something you love but it's slightly damaged, you might be able to get an extra discount. Show the damage to the cashier and ask for a marked-down price.

58 *Get* a massage

College life can take a toll on your body. Between enduring academic stress, typing at a computer, sleeping on an uncomfortable dorm room mattress, carrying piles of books, and playing intramural sports, you have a lot of reasons to be sore.

When it comes to sore or stiff muscles, there's nothing more relaxing than a good massage. A nice rubdown can soothe anxiety, ease pain, and loosen tension. A masseuse can tell you where your problem areas are and recommend better habits: "Don't carry all your books in your purse over one shoulder." "Stop sleeping with your biology textbook under your pillow. It's bad for your neck."

Don't mind needles?

Acupuncture is another form of body therapy in which acupuncturists insert thin needles into specific points in your skin. The method is used to treat lower-back pain, migraines, menstrual cramps, and more. If you're not afraid of needles and want to try an intense, time-honored treatment, acupuncture might be for you.

➤ HOW TO DO IT

There are many, many kinds of massages, and not every kind is right for every person. Here are some of the most common types:

➤ Swedish massage: A flowing, gentle full-body massage intended for relaxation.

➤ Trigger-point massage: Focuses specifically on sensitive, tight muscle fibers that can trigger pain elsewhere. It's good if you have specific areas of pain, instead of all-over soreness.

- Deep-tissue massage: Targets deep muscles and tissue. Recommended for those who prefer hard massage, this type is great for injury recovery.

- Sports massage: Specifically tailored to sports and sports injuries.

- Shiatsu massage: Intense finger or palm pressure is used to relieve tension or pain in nerves and muscles.

After you choose the type of massage you want, look at your options in town, read consumer reviews, and ask friends for recommendations. Massages at spas or other fancy places can be expensive, so if you're on a tight budget, check if massage schools offer discount rates. Massage students need to practice, and they might as well practice on you!

Every state has strict massage-therapy licensing laws, and going to an unqualified therapist can lead to injury. So do the research and choose wisely!

When you get a massage, tell the masseuse if you have any injuries or areas that need special attention. Don't be shy about asking for a harder or softer touch. You don't want to leave the table unsatisfied!

59 *Indulge* in an all-day TV marathon

For some, an all-day TV marathon is already on the schedule every Saturday. But for those who have never experienced the lazy glory of a TV marathon, you're missing out on some serious relaxation. You've spent endless hours studying, going to the gym, and managing your everyday college life. It wouldn't hurt *just once* to have one nonstop, guilt-free TV marathon, would it? You could catch up on all the shows everyone's been talking about, watch all the Harry Potter or Jason Bourne movies, or just veg out to cartoons all day.

Whatever your preference, there's nothing quite like an all-day TV marathon to make you feel truly relaxed and seriously spoiled. You've been working hard—you deserve it!

The five steps to the perfect TV marathon pose

1 / Sit on couch.

2 / Surround self with an inordinate amount of pillows.

3 / Lounge. Lounge hard.

4 / Stare blankly. Drool slightly.

5 / Create semipermanent indent in couch.

Voilà! You're a master!

➤ HOW TO DO IT

1 / If you don't have a TV, arrange an indulgence date with a friend who does.

2 / Fill up your Netflix queue, stockpile your favorite DVDs, select your on-demand shows, or, if all else fails, watch regular TV. (There's sure to be a *Law & Order* marathon on some channel.) One option is to watch an entire series in succession. This requires less thinking, and by all means, you should not be thinking.

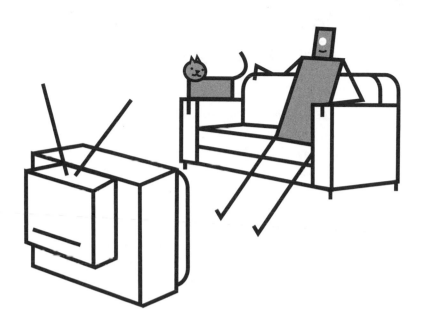

3 / Stock up on junk food. Also, regular food doesn't hurt.

4 / Wear comfortable clothes. *Really* comfortable clothes, like pajamas or your ugliest sweatpants. You're going to be wearing them all day long.

5 / Ignore your phone.

6 / If you start to feel traces of guilt or shame, ignore them! Switch the DVD or channel, enjoy the pitter-patter of rain outside, and feel sorry for all your friends who are busy moving around. No guilt allowed.

7 / Repeat steps 4 through 6, all day long.

8 / Pass out.

9 / Wake up at an odd hour a little disoriented.

10 / You're done! Now take a shower, get out of the house, and do something.

Have a shameless junk food night

You've been going to the gym a few times a week. You've been watching what you eat with an eagle eye, choosing salads over sundaes and taking in veggies with a vengeance. You feel energized, healthy, and happy with your body.

If you've been taking good care of yourself, you're due for a treat! While junk food–packed evenings are not a good idea on a regular basis, everyone deserves a guilty pleasure feast now and then. If you feel you've earned the right to go overboard, go for it. You can get back in the saddle tomorrow. (You might never want to see sugar again after this!)

➤ HOW TO DO IT

You can schedule a junk food night for any reason—a breakup, an unexpected A on your physics exam, or a rare get-together with a friend—or for no reason at all. Whatever reason you choose, a junk food night should be treated as a very special occasion. You *could* just grab some potato chips and candy bars from the dorm vending machine, but why not get creative? Why not arrange an *entire meal* based around the food you rarely allow yourself to binge on?

Here's a suggested menu for your junk food feast. Find recipes online and make these foods yourself, or feel free

> ### Okay, okay: disclaimer
>
> Don't indulge in this kind of thing if you have food-related health problems like diabetes or if you overeat regularly. Also, don't do it if you need tons of energy the next day— like for a big game or a test. A junk food night is a treat, so be sure to treat it that way.

to buy them premade at the store. Do whatever feels junkier. Invite friends to help you chow down, because it's not easy, or advisable, to eat this much food on your own!

Menu

Mac-and-cheese balls

Corn dogs

Biscuits 'n' gravy

Banana-Nutella empanadas

Milkshakes

And for dessert, some good, old-fashioned chocolate chip cookies!

61 *Get* a facial

You only have one face, and it's important to take care of it. Your face makes your first impression upon the world, and it can show people whether you're feeling confident and attractive or totally crappy. Do yourself a favor and treat your lovely face to some pampering by getting a facial.

Facials include a range of skin treatments that deep-clean, moisturize, rejuvenate, and heal your skin, whether it's dry, oily, blemished, or scarred. You won't leave a facial with completely perfect skin or a cure to serious skin problems, but you will leave feeling like your face is healthy and radiant. A good facial might even inspire you to get facials and skin treatments more often, which *will* lead to better long-term skin health.

➤ HOW TO DO IT

Skin is a complicated and delicate organ, so make sure you're going to a licensed aesthetician, not an amateur, if you're planning on paying for a facial. Keep in mind that you can also customize your facial. Spas usually offer a few kinds of facials specialized for certain types of skin. The aesthetician should be able to tell you which facial would be best for your skin, but you should at least be familiar with the options before your appointment.

For the dudes: the straight-razor shave

If you've got facial hair and have zero interest in facials, a close shave can yield some of the same results of a facial. Your skin will feel smooth, soft, and free of irritation. The classic shave is a somewhat forgotten art, but more and more barber shops and specialty grooming stores offer straight-razor shaves. After going to a real pro, you may never pick up a disposable razor again.

If you don't want to splurge on a professional facial, you can do your own at home. DIY facials usually start with a deep-cleansing wash, followed by applying a mixture rich in vitamins.

Here's one recipe for a coffee facial, adapted from *Girl in a Fix: Quick Beauty Solutions (and Why They Work)* by Somer Flaherty and Jen Kollmer:

Save the grounds from your coffee pot and use them for an energizing facial.

1 / Combine ¼ cup of cooled coffee grounds with one egg white.

2 / Massage the mixture into your skin and let it dry on your face.

3 / Leave the mixture on your face for about 15 to 20 minutes.

4 / Rinse your face and finish with your favorite moisturizer.

The coffee grounds act as an exfoliant, while the egg white helps the mixture hold together as it dries. The caffeine in the coffee grounds also helps firm and tighten your skin.

62 *Pimp* your ride

One way or another, you have to get from point A to point B. Whether you have a car, a bike, a longboard, or the shoes on your feet, something is helping you move—and it probably could use an upgrade. That upgrade can be completely utilitarian, like a tune-up or oil change, or as fun, eye-catching, and frivolous as you like.

Upgrading your ride will liven up any commute. Whether you spring for nicer hubcaps the next time you get your tires rotated or add streamers to your bike handlebars (just like back in second grade), you'll enjoy getting from place to place more if you like how you're getting there. You don't need to be crafty to show your mode of transportation some love. And one way or another, the additional effort will make you one proud commuter.

➤ HOW TO DO IT

Need a place to start? Here are some ideas for upgrading a few modes of transportation.

Embellishing your shoes (for the pedestrian in all of us)

➤ Dye your leather shoes a darker color using shoe polish or shoe dye.

➤ Paint on your shoe surface with acrylic paint. You can do this easily on canvas shoes, or on your leather shoes after you scrub out the shine with some acetone.

➤ Take your shoes to a cobbler or shoe repair shop to breathe life into a broken heel or worn-out sole.

Thinking bigger?

Maybe you're going to a festival or costume party, or maybe you're just a serious exhibitionist and you *really* want to draw attention to your transportation. Most of the suggestions here are small DIY projects, but if you're thinking bigger (and you've got money to burn), the sky's the limit. From adding spoilers to your car to building a completely bedazzled, glow-in-the-dark, flamethrowing bike from scratch, you can consult with sculptors, designers, welders, cosmetic mechanics, and a host of pros on how to go crazy. Happy crafting!

Upgrading your bike

➤ There's a lot of stuff you can add to a bike: the standard bell, a horn, a basket, or a cup holder. Just make sure the extra gear doesn't get in the way of the real gears or brakes.

➤ Your bike should already have safety lights, but you can add LED lights around the frame or on the spokes so they spin round and round. Mesmerizing . . .

➤ Bikes consist of transferable parts. Make a long-term project out of upgrading various elements, like switching out the factory-issue saddle for a suspension seat or upgrading to nicer brake pads. Consult a bike expert on what kinds of parts you should buy.

Showing your car some love

➤ Add interior decorations, like stuff hanging from the rearview mirror, seat covers in your favorite color, or LED light strips lining the car's stereo or floormats. Make sure any additions don't inhibit your view of the road or your mirrors. Safety first!

➤ Boost your stereo with new speakers, an amplifier, or a subwoofer.

➤ Paint your car, or parts of your car, any color. You can do this on a budget using paint, primer, brushes, sandpaper, trays, and some painter's tape (not to mention elbow grease). Or splurge on a visit to an auto detailer and let a professional do the work.

63 *Fly* somewhere on a budget

Ah, vacation. The smell of sunscreen, the sand, the hot bodies, the picnics, the palm trees, the hotel pool, the surfing—it's nice to daydream about these delights while you're sitting in class during a cold winter. But all this and more could be yours, just a short flight away.

Maybe you've gone on vacations with your family, or maybe you've never left your state, but you're an adult now, and you can go wherever you want! A road trip with your friends (see page 108) and studying abroad (see page 80) are good points of entry into travel. But if you want to take travel to the next level, book a flight somewhere. The beach or a ski lodge, the Caribbean warmth or Canadian slopes, are an airport away, and you can usually go on a budget. So quit daydreaming and start traveling!

➤ HOW TO DO IT

If you haven't flown often, check out these secrets to getting cheap flights.

1 / SEARCH ONLINE. Sites like Kayak.com and Priceline.com aggregate the cheapest flights available (sometimes with hotel and car-rental packages), but you can also go to individual airline websites, like Jetblue and Virgin America, to check out round-trip deals.

2 / PLAN AHEAD. The further in advance you book your tickets, the cheaper your flights usually will be.

3 / BE FLEXIBLE. The more flexible you are with flight dates and times, the cheaper the tickets will be. Also, if you're not picky about

The friend game

You know that friend who won't go anywhere without her phone, or the friend who will inevitably lose his passport and have a freakout in the airport? Leave that person at home. This is vacation, not a babysitting gig! Bring along friends who can handle the unexpected, because when traveling, it's best to expect the unexpected. Plan another activity with your higher-maintenance friends.

where you want to go, you can sign up for discount email updates from sites like Groupon, which offer vacation packages.

4 / BE PREPARED. After booking a flight, arrange for a hotel or hostel and transportation way before you depart. Do you have a friend who lives in the area you're traveling to? It's always cheaper to stay with someone you know and borrow a car if you need one.

5 / STOCK UP. Buy groceries when you get to your destination instead of indulging in fine dining every night.

6 / CHOOSE WISELY. Some places are just plain more expensive than others. A trip to Mexico City is going to be far cheaper than a trip to, say, Paris. Flying in the off-season helps, but the weather might suck, so weigh the pros and cons and take the trip that works best for you.

Once you have all the details taken care of, it's time for some hard-core relaxation. Planning a vacation isn't always easy, but at least you'll have a tan to show for it.

64 *Find* your nap time

When you were a kid, napping was a chore. For adults, napping is a luxury. A good nap will give you the energy to get through a long day and might also provide you with some surreal daytime dreams. Other mammals do it, and in some cultures, a midday siesta is an everyday occurrence. So, what's stopping you from joining the nap-time revolution?

According to the National Sleep Foundation, regular, proper napping can increase alertness, decrease the chance of making mistakes, and energize you. A study of pilots and astronauts found that a forty-minute nap improved their performance by 34 percent and their alertness by 100 percent. If a nap can help them get into space, it can help you ace that test.

Cozy up

Maybe you live in a noisy dorm, or your room is impossibly bright during the day. Limit the noise and light, but if you can't, find a place where you can. Grab a snuggly blanket and your teddy bear (you didn't leave him all alone at your parents' house, did you?), and get snoozing.

➤ HOW TO DO IT

If you've ever felt groggy after a nap, it's probably because you slept too long. A short nap of thirty to forty minutes is ideal for waking up refreshed. Be sure to set an alarm when you nap; if it takes you a while to fall asleep, make space for that extra time.

The time of day when you choose to nap is also important. A nap too late in the day might interfere with your sleep schedule (such as it is), but your body might not want a nap too early in the day. Between 2 p.m. and

5 p.m. is a pretty good range, but this depends on when you wake up and when you plan on going to bed.

What kind of a napper are you?

> ➤ Planned napper: You might take a planned nap if you know you're going to stay up late studying or hanging out with friends and want some extra energy.

> ➤ Emergency napper: Emergency napping is for situations when you can't be tired, like when you're driving or operating machinery.

> ➤ Habitual napping: A habitual napper is someone who naps at the same time every day. Lots of people were habitual nappers when they were kids, but adults can benefit from the habit, too.

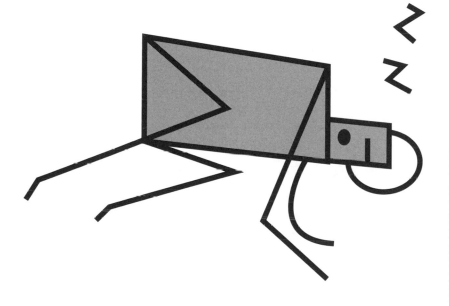

65 Break one of your own rules

Some rules are essential, like the rules we give ourselves about being true to our friends, doing well in school, and staying safe. But in some cases, breaking your own rules can feel good. If you're the type who "is always in bed at 10 p.m. sharp" or "flosses every Tuesday, Thursday, and Sunday" or "will never eat sushi," you may be abiding by rules worth breaking. Sometimes we hold on to certain rules because we were raised with them or we're used to them, not because they necessarily apply anymore. Strict rules divide things into black and white, but the real world is made up of shades of gray, and if you're too strict about rules, you'll never find out if you should keep them or not.

Rules worth breaking

"I clean every night of the week, no exception."

"I can't sing. I'll never do karaoke."

"I hate country music."

"I could never wear that."

"I have to be the smartest one in the room, always."

"I don't eat spicy food."

"I'd never survive in the big city."

➤ HOW TO DO IT

Figure out what your rules are. You might not realize that you *have* rules, because you're so used to them. Think of your phobias, your pet peeves, and all the times you've said no when you could have said yes (or vice versa) without serious consequences. Chances are that some sort of "rule" you've made for yourself is causing you to make the decisions you're making.

Consider all the things you supposedly "hate," or "would never do" or (alternatively) "would always do," and ask yourself if there's a really, really good reason behind it, or if you can afford to relax your standards just a little bit—even if only once. If you let go for a bit, you might find that the rule isn't for you anymore.

Of course, this does *not* apply to unsafe situations or the rules of your school. Don't drink an entire keg if you've been sober all your life, don't break dorm regulations, and don't eat food you're allergic to—those kinds of rules exist for a reason.

66 At the end of your rope?
Take time off from school

School is stressful. Between schoolwork, social life, living in a new location, and possible financial pressures, you're taking on a lot. If the stress is getting to be too much and you aren't enjoying your experience, you might consider taking time off from school.

Many universities are flexible about students taking entire semesters or years off. You can use the time to regroup, start a new project, relax, heal from injuries or a family crisis, travel, "figure it all out"—whatever you need. This is a great opportunity to give yourself a break without doing something drastic like dropping out.

Taking time off will probably delay your graduation date, but it won't impact your GPA—or your future career, unless you decide never to go back to school. Temporary withdrawal isn't for everyone, but students do it all the time and return to school right as rain.

Time off before you start

Some colleges recommend that students take time off *before* they start school. Harvard University says fifty to seventy students defer enrollment in their first year and wind up doing fulfilling activities, like traveling or volunteering. The university says that deferring does not affect their academic progress. If you have the option to defer enrollment after you've been accepted to college, take it under consideration.

➤ HOW TO DO IT

Take your time deciding whether time off is right for you. Don't do it on impulse; if you're having a particularly bad week, maybe things will blow over by the next week. However, if staying in school will affect your long-term well-being and academic performance, time off might be right for you.

If so, plan in advance. Visit your dean or advisor to get all the information you need. Understand that you probably won't have the same access to room, board, dining hall discounts, and other student privileges. You'll need to know where you're going to live and how you'll be supported, even if you are heading back to your folks' place. If you're on scholarship or financial aid, make sure that taking time off won't jeopardize it.

Taking a break is always better than leaving entirely. Give yourself space to reevaluate, and then make an informed decision when you're in a better mental and emotional place.

SEVEN For the Future

Build your résumé

You don't have to be a seasoned job seeker to know that every employer—from a coffee shop owner to a corporate manager—wants to see a résumé. Even in informal cases when a friend of a friend is going to "put in a good word for you," you should pass along a résumé. It's standard in the professional world, and it's a handy summary of your goals and experience.

A résumé, or a CV (the initials stand for "curriculum vitae"), which is pretty much just a longer, more detailed version of a résumé, is the most important document you have in your job search. It's usually the first impression you make on an employer, and it can be your gateway to an interview or your gateway to the rejection pile. A résumé should offer a quick, easy-to-read summary of your qualifications, education, special skills, and goals. It can also say other, more subtle things about you: a sloppy, poorly formatted, or overly busy résumé may make you look unqualified for some jobs, while a stark, boring résumé might not work for some potential employers.

Be Bobby Eager

Here's a sample résumé you can use as a template. Meet the fictitious Bobby Eager.

Bobby Eager
Mannfield College Address
PO Box 529
Springfield, TX 00021
bobby.eager@hireme.com
www.bobbyiseager.com

Objective: I am aiming to develop and nurture my career as a writer.

WORK EXPERIENCE

Internship, The Mannfield Publishing House   7/2012–present
- Read three manuscripts per week and offered feedback to editorial director
- Scouted new writers for the nonfiction division
- Entered sales data for the company's 7,000 active publications

Sports Writer, The Morris High School Weekly   2009–2011
- Reported news and wrote regular features on all Morris High School sports

Volunteer, Morris Soup Kitchen   2006–2010
- Aided soup kitchen staff with cooking, cleaning, and serving every Saturday
- Advised local homeless teens on returning to high school

EDUCATION

Mannfield College
Major: Journalism
Graduation Date: May 2014
Course Highlights: Journalism, News Reporting, English, American History, Anthropology 101

SPECIAL SKILLS

Photoshop, HTML, WordPress, Microsoft Office, conversational Italian

➤ HOW TO DO IT

1 / KNOW THE BASICS. There are many résumé templates, but as you've probably learned in school, the simplest includes a header with name and contact information; objective; work, volunteer, or internship experience (with the most recent and relevant job listed up top); education; and, lastly, extra skills, like Photoshop or proficiency in Spanish.

2 / KEEP IT SHORT. A résumé should be close to one page. This may mean doing some judicious trimming. Include your most relevant and recent experience and skills, and save the interesting anecdotes for your cover letter or interview.

3 / EVERYTHING COUNTS! Under each job you list as work experience, briefly outline what you did. Even if a task felt silly and inconsequential, it developed a skill that's an asset to you now. If you did a bit of tweeting or Facebooking on behalf of your college theater department, it's fair to say that you "Coordinated social media across platforms." Sounds great.

4 / KEEP IT CLEAN. Some people use colors, borders, and unique formatting to spruce up a résumé, and very often, these extras work wonders. The trick is to make your résumé look nice without messing with the rules listed above. You don't want the design of your résumé to distract an employer from your qualifications.

5 / NO TYPOS! Always proofread your résumé for mistakes before you send it. If you can, have a friend look over it, too. The more eyes searching for mistakes, the more you're likely to catch.

6 / SPREAD IT AROUND. In addition to the PDF or Word document you send to potential employers, you should make your résumé available online. Upload your info to the appropriate job sites (keeping information like your address private, of course), and post your résumé on LinkedIn.com and on your personal website, if you have one.

68 *Build* a website

A personal website is handy for any growing professional. If you're in a visual industry like art or design or a tech-based industry, or if you have a lot to show for your work over the years, you might want to build a website of your own. You can use the website to store your work samples, photos, résumé, contact information, and blog, all in one place. A website is also a great way to optimize your Google-ability: people who search your name online will probably see your website first, instead of your Facebook page or a link to an article about your high school swim team.

➤ HOW TO DO IT

1 / DETERMINE THE MAIN PURPOSE.
Is the website a place to house all your writing samples? A home for your blog or franchise? A visual portfolio? A how-to site with tons of videos and demonstrations? These distinctions will dictate what kind of site to build and what features to include.

2 / BROWSE AROUND. Pick a handful of personal sites with elements that you like. A sculptor's site might be attractive, but if you're in a different industry, some aspects won't be appropriate for you. Choose the design elements that will work best for your site. As a general rule, your site should be clean, professional, and easy to navigate.

Go SEO!

When you Google something, do you go for the first result or the five hundredth? If you're like most people, you probably go for the first result. How did that result get to be number one? It's probably because of SEO.

SEO, or search engine optimization, is a method of making your website more visible on search engines. It's especially important if you're in a competitive industry or have a very common name. There are many tricks to improving your SEO. You can use popular keywords and phrases in your site, link to other pages and websites frequently, and name your pages with distinctive title tags. SEO might sound complicated, but once you read a few tutorials, you'll find that it's actually pretty intuitive. You can use services like Google Analytics to track your website traffic and your placement in Google search results.

3 / IF YOU'RE NEW TO WEB DESIGN, FIND A TEMPLATE YOU CAN BUY OR USE FOR FREE. Sites like WordPress.com and Blogger have templates that are easy for beginners to navigate and tweak and can be upgraded later for a fee.

4 / DESIGN YOUR SITE. If you have time and you're interested in design, play around with the template and features of your website. If you're uncomfortable messing around with HTML, you might want to hire a professional designer or tech-savvy friend to do the heavy lifting for you.

5 / PICK A GREAT DOMAIN NAME! Choose a URL that clearly states your name or project and isn't hard to remember. If you're using a free platform like WordPress or Blogger, you might have some restrictions on the domain name you can choose. If you feel strongly about a certain domain name, you can purchase it from a site like GoDaddy.com.

69 *Get* an internship

These days, internships are a crucial step in launching a career. Unless you're lucky enough to have a job waiting for you once you graduate from college, an internship is a natural stepping stone into your chosen path. An internship can be a practical way to learn skills in your chosen trade and get a feel for what the real workforce is like without the commitment of a full-time job, and you may even get college credit. It's also a great way to get your foot in the door for paid opportunities later on. You might be making spreadsheets and opening the mail now, but many companies hire from their intern pool.

Working for free might be a financial burden (though there are those rare paid internships), but the experience you'll gain will be priceless.

➤ HOW TO DO IT

To find an internship, visit your school's career development department. The staff will probably ask you what industry you're interested in and point you in the direction of companies they recommend or have connections with.

If the career development department is a dead end, look on your own. Just like finding a job, scoring an internship is a matter of establishing personal connections, doing some research, and applying to anything and everything that sounds remotely interesting. Many large companies have online internship application forms. Smaller companies often list a contact person on their website, so research the companies you're interested in and contact them accordingly.

Know your rights

Unfortunately, some companies exploit their interns by using them as employees—without the pay. Believe it or not, there are laws out there to protect you from this kind of exploitation. The US Fair Labor Standards Act is in place to help people understand the basic legal parameters of an internship. Using them as a resource, a fair internship looks like this:

* The internship, even though it includes actual operation of the employer's facilities, is similar to training that would be given in an educational environment.

* The internship experience is for the benefit of the intern.

* The intern does not displace regular employees, but works under close supervision of existing staff.

* The employer that provides the training derives no immediate advantage from the intern's activities, and on occasion, its operations may actually be impeded.

* The intern is not necessarily entitled to a job at the conclusion of the internship.

* The employer and the intern understand that the intern is not necessarily entitled to wages for the time spent in the internship.

Once you're in the door, treat your internship like a paying job. Be on time, work hard, and make as many connections as possible. If you have ideas to contribute or think you can help with a project you aren't assigned to, tell your supervisor. It's up to you to make the most of your internship, so be proactive and willing to assist with whatever task you're assigned to.

70 *Improve* your social media presence

Even if you haven't created a personal website, you're probably on Facebook, Twitter, Instagram, or some other form of social media. These days, social media isn't only a way to engage with friends; it's also a tool to connect with the world, promote yourself, and maybe even gain employment.

Some employers will look at your social media profiles to get a larger picture of who you are. Twitter and Facebook may not be the same as a job interview, but social media is one way you present yourself to the world. When you're starting out in your career, social media, used correctly, can be a helpful tool you can use to your advantage.

➤ HOW TO DO IT

1 / **CLEAN IT UP.** Don't put anything online that you wouldn't want an employer to see.

2 / **SWEAR OFF BAD HABITS.** No more engaging in petty Twitter wars, posting incriminating photos on Instagram (read: keg stands and bongs), publicly trolling, or gossiping online. If you have bad social media habits like these, now's the time to swear off them off for good.

3 / **UPDATE IT.** Make sure your Facebook, LinkedIn, and Twitter profiles, for example, are complete with information about your interests, professional experience, and education. This also goes for any social media site that might be relevant to your field. If you're a musician looking for commercial attention, you'll want a complete a Sound-Cloud profile, for example.

To brand or not to brand

You might have heard the word *branding* thrown around in marketing classes or social circles. In a social media context, *branding* basically means using social media to promote the Empire of You. The budding writer. The socialite. The future psychologist. If you're the entrepreneurial type, branding can be a productive way to give your web presence a coherent focus, but it isn't entirely necessary this early in your career. If branding comes easily to you, go for it. If not, there's time for that later.

4 / FOLLOW AND FRIEND. Build up your network by connecting with relevant industry professionals and figures on the social media sites they use.

5 / KEEP IT GOING. Regularly post on your social media profiles. Don't post so much that you annoy people, but post enough so that you build an online presence. Use posts to promote your own stuff, engage people in conversation, share links, and show your personality.

71 *Get* an interview outfit

Whether you've landed a job interview at a bar or a bank, you should look your best. Even if your potential job or internship comes with a casual dress code, showing up to the interview in nice clothes is good form. A well-chosen outfit indicates respect, class, and professionalism—all the things an employer wants to see.

There's something satisfying about buying an outfit with the sole purpose of wearing it to an interview. You *could* cobble something together from the clothes you already have, but confidence is key in an interview, and getting a new outfit that screams "HIRE ME!" and makes you feel like a million bucks—even if it cost twenty—is definitely a worthwhile investment.

➤ HOW TO DO IT

An interview outfit is a whole head-to-toe package: proper shoes, skirt or pants, shirt or dress, and maybe a tie or accessories. You don't have to splurge on a completely new set of clothes. Thrift stores like Goodwill and the Salvation Army carry lots of professional clothes that will impress any employer.

In most cases, go for something simple. You want a potential employer to notice you, not your outfit. The exception would be if you're interviewing for a high-end fashion job or at a totally hip place that values individualism and especially creative choices.

Here are some general dos and don'ts:

➤ **DOS:** blazer, long skirt or dress, slacks, suit, black tights, low heels, dressy boots, dress shoes, tie, stylish accessory like a tie clip or a brooch

➤ **DON'TS:** flip-flops, jeans, sneakers, superhigh heels, low-cut shirt, shorts, short skirt or dress, distracting colors, beachwear, hat, fishnet tights, cargo pants

Talk to the hair

Your hair is also a crucial part of your look. For your job interview, keep your hair neat and unobtrusive. If you have long hair, put it up, and don't use tons of product or accessorize too much. Like your outfit, your hair should go relatively unnoticed.

72 *Become* financially empowered

I f you're like most college students, you probably don't have many assets. But whether you have a lot of money or a little, knowing about your finances and managing them well are essential parts of adult life.

Financial empowerment is about knowing your options, setting goals, and being realistic about your finances. Unfortunately, personal finance isn't covered much in school—gone are the days of learning to balance a checkbook in home ec class—and many college students flounder, panic, and bury their heads in the sand when it comes to cash and credit.

However, anyone can learn about personal finance and get on the right track. By educating yourself on a few ins and outs, you'll feel much more comfortable about your financial future, no matter what fiscal circumstances you encounter.

➤ HOW TO DO IT

1 / Assess your current situation honestly and frankly by answering a few questions.

➤ How much money are you making on your own or getting from your family each month?

> What are your essential monthly expenses (food, rent, transportation, phone, loans, school books, credit card debt)?

> What do you have left over after expenses, if anything?

2 / Consider what you could do differently. Maybe your assessment shows that you need more money to sustain yourself. In this case, a higher-paying part-time job or signing up for another student loan should be your goal. Or maybe you have more money left over each month than you thought, but you're throwing the extra cash away on expensive dinners, movies, and clothes. In that case, cut down your expenses and start setting aside some savings.

The idea is to get to a point where you can start saving, even a bit at a time. Once you get a regular salary, you can put money in a savings account weekly or monthly. No matter how big or small your salary is, depositing into a savings account regularly will add up.

73 *Get* a part-time job

The truth is that part-time jobs can be a pain. Unless you're lucky to land a position (or a paid internship) in the industry of your choice, part-time jobs in college usually involve doing something you wouldn't otherwise do unless you were being paid, like serving food in a restaurant until midnight or waking up at 7 a.m. on a Saturday to mow someone's lawn. However, part-time jobs build character, they show an excellent work ethic on your résumé, and, oh yeah, they allow you to make money. You'll be able to spring for those new shoes you've been drooling about for months without any help from anyone (or for those new textbooks, depending on how strapped for cash you are). How awesome would that feel?

Some part-time gigs can be particularly gratifying or, at least, lucrative. Jobs like babysitting, waiting tables, filing, retail, or work on campus can lead to new friends, new skills, and a decent salary. You might gain networking opportunities, too. You never know—that customer at table three might be the employer of your dreams.

Work-study

If you're on financial aid and meet certain parameters, you might be eligible for work-study. Work-study is a program in which the federal government pays part of a student's salary. Work-study students usually get first dibs on jobs, since the employer only has to pay half of the salary. Ask the financial aid office if you're eligible for work-study.

➤ HOW TO DO IT

One of the first steps is to visit your school's career development center. This is a good resource for opportunities on campus, such as manning a front desk, working in the dining hall, or doing clerical work.

Some schools also have agencies that connect students directly to outside employers. A school babysitting agency, for example, connects college sitters to needy parents in the community. Some schools also have bartending or catering businesses that connect bartenders and catering staff to community events.

You can also inquire at establishments outside school by scouring job ads online, on storefronts, and in newspapers and hitting up your contacts. Be aware: Many off-campus employers can't be sympathetic to your class schedule, so make sure that the job isn't going to interfere with school before you accept it.

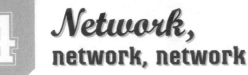

74 *Network,* network, network

The connections you make now will last a lifetime if you nurture those relationships. Imagine if you put effort into initiating new contacts every day. Over the course of a year, your address book will be overflowing!

Many people get jobs through connections and internal contacts at companies. Networking is almost as important as simply graduating from college.

Even if some of your contacts can't help you now, they might be essential in the future. Once you graduate, you can hit up your contacts for job openings. Or, when you need to find a good financial adviser, you can ask your finance friend for a referral. Or, when you're looking for a new apartment, you can contact that friend who became a real estate agent. See how it works?

➤ HOW TO DO IT

Here are some general guidelines for building your base.

1 / BE OUT AND ABOUT. Show up to events in town, especially if they relate to your industry.

2 / TALK TO PEOPLE. A good networker is assertive but not annoying. Approach people when they aren't otherwise occupied. Tell them honestly what you're about, even if you're just a floundering college student looking to meet people. Ask plenty of sincere questions. People like flattery, but not if it seems desperate or forced.

3 / EXCHANGE CONTACT INFORMATION. Have a business card handy, and never leave a helpful conversation without getting contact information—or at least full names so you can friend people on Face-

How to make a business card

Business cards are easy and relatively cheap to make these days. You can go to websites like Vistaprint.com and have lots of personalized cards printed for a very small fee. A business card should include your name, some sort of a title (even if it's something like "writer of all trades" or "your all-purpose graphics guy"), and any contact information (phone number, email address, or website).

book or connect on LinkedIn. If they're reluctant to give you the info, take the hint and let it go.

4 / FUEL THE FLAME. Networking is reciprocal. If you scratch other people's backs, they'll scratch yours. Stay in contact with people in your network, and help them whenever you can.

5 / DON'T BURN BRIDGES. The working world is much smaller than you might think, and you don't want anyone out there sabotaging you. Even if you really, really dislike someone, do everything you can to stay on good terms.

Forgive your own mistakes

You will inevitably make mistakes in college. Maybe you stayed up too late and slept through an important exam. Or you fell deeply into debt or embarrassed yourself at a party. Perhaps you lost a good friend. Maybe you'll look back and realize you picked the wrong major, or you regret partying too much and studying too little (or vice versa).

These sorts of mistakes aren't fun to live with, but they are a part of life, and everybody, *everybody*, makes them.

Mistakes don't end up being as catastrophic as they seem at the time you make them, so don't be too hard on yourself. If you wade in shame and let your mistakes hold you back from living your life, you'll be missing out on a lot of good stuff. Forgiving your mistakes is key to becoming a successful human being.

Got a record?

Some mistakes have graver consequences than others. If you've committed a crime, you may be able to forgive yourself emotionally, but your record can mess with employment opportunities for the rest of your life. In some cases, however, you might be able to expunge your record or reduce the charges. Find out your state's policy on expunging criminal records, and do everything you can to get a clean slate.

➤ HOW TO DO IT

1 / RECTIFY WHAT YOU CAN. End that bad relationship. Set a plan to get out of debt, even if it will take years to complete. Make apologies.

2 / HINDSIGHT REALLY IS 20/20. If we had hindsight *all* the time, we wouldn't make any mistakes to begin with. If you're looking back on some decisions as mistakes, remember that you were probably in a different mind-set and had a different motivation when you made them. Part of forgiving yourself is realizing that mistakes are a part of growth and change and that they're not always avoidable.

3 / MOVE ON. In some cases, there's nothing you can do but get up off the ground and keep going. Dwelling on the past will get you nowhere. As an adult, you can reinvent yourself as many times as you want, so pick yourself up, dust off, and start a new chapter!

76 *Keep* your good friends

True friends really do last a lifetime. Many people keep their childhood or college friends well into adulthood and even into old age. After you graduate, you'll share an important bond with the friends you knew during your formative years, and you don't want to let them disappear from your life.

College is a special time when you're surrounded by people who are close to your own age, interested in the things you're interested in (for the most part), and looking to make new friends as much as you are. But after college, you'll be part of a more diverse population with varying goals and interests, and it can be harder to make quick, lasting connections. For these reasons and more, it's crucial to keep the good friends you have. They could be part of your support structure for the rest of your life.

➤ HOW TO DO IT

You'll make tons of acquaintances in college. You'll meet people in class, at parties, and in extracurricular activities, memorize hundreds of names, and say yes to a lot of friend requests. But at the end of the day, who are your *real* friends?

Your real friends are the supremely loyal ones. They're the ones you can trust. They're the ones you feel completely connected to on a deep level, even when they're not around.

Your truest friends will be there for you when you're in a tough place. It's easy to be nice to someone at a party, but a true friend will be around through thick and thin. If you go through a devastating break-up or the loss of a family member, a true friend will be by your side, helping you back on your feet. The acquaintances will probably vanish.

How to spot a fair-weather friend

Think that dude or lady is a friend? Here are the signs to watch for in fake friends:

* They only call when they need something.

* They disappear for long stretches of time—then reappear, acting as if nothing happened.

* They're not really interested in you (aside from what you have to offer them).

* They act like you have a much deeper connection than you actually do.

* They're *never* there when you really need a friend.

Once you recognize who your true friends are, make an effort to stay in touch with them. Connect every now and again on the phone, over email, or face to face. Make an investment in a true friendship, because you'll need each other after you graduate.

77 Go with your gut

Making decisions is a part of life, no matter what age you are. You'll decide where to live, if you want to have children, what jobs to take, who to date, what to have for lunch, and much, much more. But with decision-making comes uncertainty. Your parents have an opinion. Your friends have an opinion. Social pressures tell you to do one thing, while other pressures tell you to do another. You shouldn't completely ignore these pressures—sometimes parents and friends have excellent advice—but you shouldn't throw away your instincts based on what other people tell you.

People make the most colossal mistakes when they don't trust their gut. They get into careers they don't enjoy, they date people they know they shouldn't, and after a while, they can start to have regrets. So get in the habit of trusting your gut in college to ensure your best possible future.

➤ HOW TO DO IT

You should know by now how it feels when your gut is telling you something. Beneath all the self-doubt and outside forces, there's a voice screaming at you, saying what is best for you. Don't ignore it!

Here are a few examples of good instincts gone to waste.

➤ "Man, I've always wanted to be the Next Great American Writer, but there's no money in it, and it's such a stupid dream. I'll just go ahead and major in business instead. I'll make more money, my parents will be happy, and I'll be taken more seriously." (This might be taken directly from Ebenezer Scrooge's autobiography.)

The myth of total, complete happiness

The myth of total happiness trips a lot of people up. Some people might tell you that you can achieve total happiness all the time (lie!) and that you can follow one streamlined way to get there (another lie!). The truth is that there are millions of ways to live your life, and all of them will be difficult at times. We can only do the best we can, so what's the point of listening to anything *but* your gut?

- ➤ "My relationship is making me miserable, but if I just hang on a little longer, I can work it out. No one will ever love me like my partner does." (Not true. You probably already have friends and family who love you very much.)

- ➤ "My roommate wants to throw a party in the dorm. Every night of the week. I have a lot of studying to do and could really use some quiet time, but I don't want to be a tight-ass." (Have fun getting written up for drinking, and getting a C on your paper.)

From the outside, it's easy to see how these thoughts are wasteful. You're rooting for the frustrated writer to go for her dream, you want the self-doubter to ditch that loser, and you want the wild child in the next room to take things down a notch (or twelve) and tell his roommate to go to a bar instead. Think about how these scenarios might apply to your own life, and take your own advice for once! Life is too short for you to be trapped.

Resources

Hopefully this book has inspired you to try a few new things and made you curious about a whole lot more. And although we didn't want to overwhelm you earlier, we thought it might be helpful here to provide a list of additional resources—including websites, apps, blogs, and social networks—in case you are interested in learning a bit more about music production, say, but don't know quite where to start.

There's a ton of information out there on whatever may have piqued your interest, but this should at least provide a place—or places—to start.

➤ WEBSITES

About.com: Beauty (Beauty.about.com)
Tips and tricks for keeping your skin radiant, including different kinds of homemade facemasks for every skin type.

A.V. Club (AVClub.com)
Filled with reviews, interviews, and film lists to help you choose just the right movie for your big night in.

Do Something DoSomething.org/actnow/actionguide/how-get-involved-local-politics
Find advice on how to get involved, information on your local senators and congressman, as well as tips on how to write a letter to an elected official.

4 Creating A Website (4CreatingAWebsite.com)
Tips and tricks for creating a first-time user-friendly website.

Go Ask Alice (Goaskalice.columbia.edu)
A website sponsored by Columbia University devoted to answering students most personal and pertinent questions—anonymously! (As well as other health information and resources.)

Homeless Shelter Directory (HomelessShelterDirectory.org)
This website provides a good resource for finding homeless shelters, free clinics, and food pantries in your area.

Intern Match (InternMatch.com)

Easy-to-use website with job and internship postings, sorted by city and industry.

Join A Campaign (JoinACampaign.com)

Allows campaigns to post job and volunteer opportunities. You can also post your own campaigns and find others to help support your cause.

Kick Starter (KickStarter.com)

You can post your project online and get donations from the citizens of the World Wide Web. If you reach your goal . . . you keep the money!

Local Harvest (LocalHarvest.com)

A handy one-stop site to search for farmers' markets in your area.

MAKE Magazine (Makezine.com)

A magazine and website devoted to helping you "make" anything and everything you can dream up, from a cool LED clock to a crocheted blanket.

The Mayo Clinic (MayoClinic.org)

An amazing resource for any and all of your health questions. They also have a convenient app you can download straight to your smartphone or tablet.

Mint (Mint.com)

Aggregates all of your personal finances into one place and allows you to track your spending, set budgets and goals, and more. There is also a complimentary app that allows you to access information from your smartphone.

My Perfect Resume (MyPerfectResume.com)

Helps you with each step of the resume-building process . . . for FREE!

National Outdoor Leadership School (NOLS.edu)

A school, based in Wyoming, dedicated to wilderness education. They offer year-round classes and adventures throughout the country.

No Nonsense Self-Defense (NoNonsenseSelfDefense.com/pyramid.html)

No-nonsense information on how to keep you and your belongings safe.

Roadtrippers (Roadtrippers.com)

Plan your whole route online with this helpful website, which also suggests fun and interesting things to do along the way.

Roaming Hunger (RoamingHunger.com)
Food trucks are a fun and cheap way to try new cuisines. This website has maps that help you find where the food trucks are serving in your city.

Rosetta Stone (RosettaStone.com)
If you don't have time for a class, language-learning software is a great (and sometimes less expensive) way to learn a new language on your own time.

Semester At Sea (SemesterAtSea.com)
A study-abroad opportunity, sponsored by the University of Virginia, that offers semester-long academic adventures.

Shutterfly (Shutterfly.com)
This website allows you to organize your photos into a hardcover book.

TAAZ: The Brains Behind the Beauty (Taaz.com)
Try new hairstyles and makeup on uploaded photos of yourself.

UJam (UJam.com)
A free music-production website that allows you to create your own tunes without downloading any software.

Volunteer Match (VolunteerMatch.org)
This site matches volunteers with organizations that need help.

ZogSports (ZogSports.com)
A co-ed sports league, with teams in cities across the country, that also functions as a social community and charity.

ZOZI Getaway (Zozi.com/getaways)
Sign up for weekly emails with great deals to help you see the world.

➤ BLOGS

Cooking in College (Cooking-in-College.com)
Recipes are designed with the budget- and health-conscious student in mind.

My First Apartment (MyFirstApartment.com)
A blog with lots of tips for the big move, with special sections that include "The Hunt," "Moving In," "Apt. Living," "Roommates," and "Money."

Small Kitchen College (College.biggirlssmallkitchen.com)
A blog with lots of ideas for fun dinner themes and recipes.

➤ APPS

CheckPlease Lite
A free app that allows you to calculate the tip for meals. It will also split the dinner check up to 100 ways.

Chegg Flashcards
Create your own flashcards or download premade flashcard sets from Quizlet.

Couch to 5K
. . . in nine weeks!

GasBuddy
This app can tell you where to find the cheapest gas while you're on the **road.**

Gympact
Earn money by reaching your fitness goals!

Lose It!
Monitor your calories by keeping track of your meals and daily activity.

Nike Training Club
Compete in challenges that unlock bonus routines, recipes, and tips.

Roadside
This app reveals roadside attractions available to you on your journey.

Scoutmob
Find local goods and great deals.

Textbook Me
The Expedia for textbooks!

Zombies, Run!
Run, dodge, and escape the zombies to complete your workout.

➤ INSPIRATION & IDEAS

Pinterest
Lots of fun ideas to get you started on your dorm room renovation.

PB Dorm (PBTeen.com/pages/pbdorm)
Your one-stop shop for XL twin sheets, accent pillows, and fun stuff for your walls. Plus, get 10 percent off with your .edu email.

Nichole McCall

About the Author

Halley Bondy is a Brooklyn-based writer who has worked as a news reporter for the *Newark Star Ledger*, an arts journalist for *Back Stage*, and as editor for MTV Iggy. She is currently senior editor for Oxygen.com. She is a playwright and comedian, and the winner of the 2008 Fringe Festival NYC for Outstanding Playwright. She is the author of *Don't Sit on the Baby: The Ultimate Babysitting Guide*.